C

FORGIVEN
AND
LOVED

*Life Seized By the Power
of Divine Affection*

By Ken Dickerson

Chosen, Forgiven and Loved: Life Seized by the Power of Divine Affection
by Ken Dickerson

Inspired Press Publisher
1333 Chelsea Court
Morrow, OH 45152
www.inspiredpresspublisher.com
513-256-1792
ISBN: 978-0-692-79030-4
Library of Congress Control Number: 2016955875

Dedication

To Jeanenne, my wife, my love, my friend, my soul-mate:

Many years have quickly passed since we made our covenant before God, our families, and a few friends. I wanted to put into writing some of the things I have learned about you that I did not know or fully appreciate on that day. I want you to have this as a benchmark we can both look back to after the next twenty years, God willing.

Along with the cross, you are living proof of how much Christ loves me. You are a constant reminder of His great mercy extended to a far less than perfect man. I have been told by more than one person over the years that you are a far better woman than I deserve. I want you to know that I totally agree and that I am grateful that others have noticed.

You are a Proverbs 31 woman. Take this fact as proof that God sees you as special and has chosen to invest great gifts in you. You are the kind of woman that a young man's parents would pray for. You are honest, faithful, loyal, industrious and hospitable. You are a friend to the friendless, and you champion the cause of the meek. You cry out for justice, but always extend mercy in full measure.

You are the heart that makes our house a home. You are the soul of our family. You are a rose among male thorns. The way you care overcomes our carelessness and inspires all of us to be better people. Your spirit is what draws us back to home when we are away – even for a short while.

Not only have you won my heart, but you have also completed it. You are the balm that has healed the self-inflicted wounds of my youth. You are my soul mate and my closest, dearest friend. Stay close my love; there is no greater comfort than to know you are mine – and I am yours. I have no regrets – only gratitude.

Ken

To my children, Candace, Scott and Philip

May the One who knows me best become your greatest aspiration and your source of hope, strength and inspiration. Be filled with His presence, peace, power, purpose, provision and protection all your days. Always live your lives full of undeniable love and unending grace for you are the hope of my posterity and the objects of this father's greatest joy.

Table of Contents

Alpha

(Introduction)

I am not a theologian, never have been, never will be. I am a fortunate man, blessed beyond measure and greatly loved by the LORD, all three of Him (Father, Son and Spirit), with a powerful divine affection. This divine affection is born, not of any need on God's part (God needs nothing), but out of a divine desire to love and love greatly. After over sixty years of earthly life, I see the fruit of this divine desire in so many aspects of my life that I can scarcely contain my wonder as I continue to ask, "Why me?"

As I look back on life, I see it filled with divine appointments and human disappointments. I must declare that the wounds I have received from life have been, for the most part, self-inflicted. I see the precious gifts I have received as mostly about God's goodness rather than my greatness. I have seen success, but owe it to providence rather than my work, my talent or my influence. I have come to the conclusion that I have a Divine Benefactor who loves me with a love that I can never return in full. The only thing I have to offer Him is me, with all the quirks and defects. Some prize! But you know, it turns out that I am all He wants. Not that I am lovely, you see, but He wants me because He is lovely. Life is always all about Him – not about me.

I am a husband, father, a grandfather, a son, a brother, and a boss to more than a few folks. I am a leader with a calling, but you are too. I have influence over more than one other person. The chances are good that you do too. How can we, through our influence, move people we know closer to the One who so greatly loves us? How can we encourage others to follow Divine love's clarion call? We need to be transparent and intentional to make disciples and fulfill all the possibilities God created in us. My leadership coach challenged me to write out my vision, plan, mission, objectives, strategies, and actions to accomplish this purpose; a plan for my business and personal life, something that could be measured, evaluated, and changed, if necessary. Here's my plan:

My Vision

I see an abundant life filled with righteousness, joy and peace through the Spirit of Christ; an intentional life of purpose with my time, talent and treasure given to the cause of Christ's Kingdom.

I see a redeemed family filled with love and the unity of the mind of Christ, all living in relationships of love while serving each other and affirming our unique gifts and callings. I see covenant relationships full of tenderness and homes full of peace.

I see a business committed to the well-being of its employees and their families as well as the success of its clients by inspiring positive people to provide excellent service with exceptional care. I see an instrument of purpose, grace and provision for hundreds of families that has a worth far greater than the sum of its parts.

My Purpose

To love the Lord with all my being (heart, soul, mind, and strength) and give my body as an instrument to make peace, give grace and work mercy in the lives and hearts of my wife, my children, my family, my friends, and my community.

To lead my family and those God has entrusted to my care to abundant life through a close and intimate relationship with God through Jesus the Christ. I will lead them by serving their needs, inspiring their thinking, engaging their dreams, and laying down my life or self-interests for their well-being.

To be filled with the Spirit of Christ, exercising the gifts He has placed in me to build up His body and to serve His causes in the earth.

My Mission

I will give myself to a consistent and intentional life of prayer, meditation and study of God's word. I will choose to be still and know God as Lord, life, power, and the source of my significance, knowing that I have been chosen and given the power to become a dearly loved child of God, a child seized by the power of a great and divine affection.

I will be motivated by the love of Christ that lives in me and strengthens me to act out His love in real ways toward all of His creation.

I will be obedient to what the LORD requires of me as shared in Micah 6:8. That is:

I will live justly by telling the truth in all circumstances and dealing honestly with all of the people my path may cross regardless of their faith, race, wealth, their past or intentions. (There is freedom in the truth.)

I will love mercy by being generous with my time, talent and treasure, extending forgiveness to those I love and to those that may despitefully use me. (There is power in forgiveness.)

I will walk humbly by being transparent, not covering my faults and embracing my frailties, knowing that Christ is made strong in my weakness. (There is wisdom in humility.)

I will not be ashamed of my past knowing that every mistake, poor decision, and self-centered action is paid for by the blood of Jesus, forgiven and forgotten by God the Father. I will not be ashamed of the Good News of Jesus Christ, knowing it is the power that saves all who believe it. I will not be ashamed of who I am, knowing that I am a new creation and now carry the name of my Creator.

This book is part of my plan. One of the strategies of fulfilling my vision and mission in the lives of my family is to encourage and teach them by writing email devotions and texting daily thoughts to them. I want them to have a record of what I have come to know that is useful, meaningful and eternal. This strategy has been in place since 2013, and there are now close to one hundred of these devotionals. Although I wrote them for my family, I have received permission to share many of them with you. I have reformatted some of them and changed some names to protect the innocent (or guilty in some cases). It is a strategy of expanding my relationship with Christ to as many or as few who have an interest in living with the power of this divine affection I have come to know. Now that you know me better, I hope the rest of this book will focus on Jesus, my Brother and Lord, His Spirit, the breath and life of God in the earth, and the Father, the beginning and ending of all there is and the fountain of indescribable love.

Something in this book will help you. Something in here will encourage you. Something in here will make you sing. Something in here will make you smile. The Christian experience is not theology; it is life. It is air to breathe and bread on which to live. It is how we live in Christ and how He lives in us. It is the reality that God is good, and we are His dearly loved children. In Him, we live and move and have our significance. These pages are meant to encourage you to live His way and fulfill the possibilities God has placed in you.

In the original form of these devotions, I included the lyrics to many songs and hymns to add to a climate of worship and to support my thoughts. The process of gaining permission to use these lyrics is exhaustive and costly, so for this book I have only referred to these songs and lyrics by title and author or performer. I do encourage you to use social media and experience these great songs because they will support the things I share and they will move your spirit to worship. The rest of the song lyrics in the book are mine – shared with me by a voice soft and tender through the years – some as long as forty years ago.

These snippets and musings bear witness to life with the One, who greatly loves. In this book, I have cataloged them to support the title of this book, a title that has become my clarion call describing who I am and how I want people to remember me. When I leave this place, they will be on my tombstone in big, loud, joyful letters – **Chosen, Forgiven and Loved**.

Chosen

"I'm not saying that I have this all together, that I have it made. But I am well on my way, reaching out for Christ, who has so wondrously reached out for me."

– Paul the Apostle (Philippians 3:12 MSG)

Why Me?

Chosen

In Matthew 22 Jesus tells a story about a wedding feast the king planned for his son, sending invitations throughout his kingdom. Many guests blew off his invitation, and some of them mistreated and harmed the king's messengers sent with the invitation. The king was so furious at their disregard that he proceeded to invite many poor and disadvantaged folks who would never aspire to the king's social circle. Still, when the banquet was in progress, the king noticed a "wedding crasher" or imposter who had shown up without an invitation. The king demanded an explanation and to see his invitation, which he could not produce. The "wedding crasher" was then seized and removed from the banquet and thrown out into the night. The king commented that *"many are called, but few are chosen."*

Jesus used this parable as a reminder of how important it is to answer the RSVP when the King invites us to His home. Furthermore, He used it as a warning to those who might try to crash the banquet without proper credentials. How do we know we are the chosen?

For 2000 years, the invitation to God's family has been extended from a rugged tree on a desolate hill just outside Jerusalem. In light of all humanity, it remains a mystery that so few have answered the call. The message of God's gift of abundant and eternal life has endured all this time, yet the vast majority of humanity has not answered the call.

I call this the doctrine of exclusive inclusion. The call extends to everyone, but relatively few answer the call. What is the difference between being called and chosen? In John 12 we can see some glimpses of who are the chosen. In verse 32 Jesus says, "When I am lifted up from the earth, I will draw everyone to myself." From this passage, we can clearly learn that Jesus calls to every person from the cross.

It is important for us to understand that Jesus also stated in this chapter, specifically in verse 26, "Anyone who wants to be my disciple must follow me...And my Father will honor anyone who serves me." He also exclaims in verse 32, "Put your trust in the light while there is still time; then you will become children of the light."

The sad truth is that even after all the miracles, the resurrection of Lazarus from the dead, the triumphant praise of the crowds upon His entry into Jerusalem, verse 37 says, *"But despite all the miraculous signs Jesus had done, most of the people still did not believe in him."*

Jesus' heart was heavy at this fact, and He shouted to the crowds in verse 44, *"If you trust me, you are trusting not only me but also God, who sent me. For when you see me, you are seeing the one who sent me. I have come as a light to shine in this dark world so that all who put their trust in me will no longer remain in the dark."* In verse 50 Jesus says of His Father, *"And I know his commands lead to eternal life; so I say whatever the Father tells me to say."*

We know that we are the chosen because we say yes. We RSVP the invitation. We say yes to following Jesus; we say yes to trusting in Jesus; we say yes to His light, and we say yes to what He asks us to do. The mark of the chosen is, *we say yes.* Jesus calls from the cross, "Will you believe - will you receive?" And we say, "Yes." It is simple, but it is not easy. Salvation is free; discipleship costs everything. Jesus says, "Will you give Me all of you?" We say, "Yes." With our yes we choose Him and He chooses us. To as many as receive Him to them He gives the power to become the children of God.

Scripture:

Matthew Chapter 22

John Chapter 12

Song to Consider: "Yes Lord" - Matt Redman

My Song: I'm On the Winning Side

Teach me, Lord, to always do Your will,
No matter what problems 'round me fall.
Trusting only in Your perfect love,
Leaning always on Your mighty arms.

Oh, precious Lord, You will always hear my cry,
Your never failing promises abide.
So I'll thank You for the victory,
For the fights already won.
Praise the Lord! I know I'm on the winning side.

Oh, praise the Lord! I know I'm on the winning side -
Though the way be tough and the battle's raging high.
I will thank You for the victory,
For the fights already won.
There's no joy like being on the winning side.

Jesus, take me; with Your Spirit fill.
Make me in Your likeness by Thy will.
Keep me always in Your love and care.
With others all my faith and love to share.
(Repeat Chorus)

Prayer: Father, to Jesus' call from the cross I say "Yes." I say yes, Lord, to Your will, to Your words and to Your ways. When Your Spirit speaks to me, just like Samuel, with my whole heart I will answer yes. Call me; teach me Your ways; make me like You. I will always answer, "Yes, Lord." In Jesus' name, Amen.

A Plan… A Path… A Purpose

In May 2007, I wrote two poems for my son Philip's high school graduation. Recently, I was in his room putting some stray socks away and paused to read them again. They are still on his dresser. I asked Philip if I could share some of the first poem called "A Plan…A Path…A Purpose." You see, while I truly believe that God gave me the words especially for him, they are so applicable to all of us because Jesus values each of us immensely and sees our purpose and potential from an eternal perspective. It is easy to get caught up in how truly hard life gets at times. But if we can come to a place of rest in the fact that we are special to God and have a unique purpose, we can find the fortitude to resist feeling sorry for ourselves or doubting our purpose in the life our Heavenly Father has chosen for us. Our unique gifts can have a dramatic effect on the world around us. We can be a source of joy and delight even walking through the hard parts of life.

Let me share and comment on the three parts of this poem.

A Plan…A Path…A Purpose

Resist any thought that questions your significance!

You are a source of joy and delight to all who hold you dear.

There is a plan for your life.

> Work that only you can accomplish.
>
> Gifts that only you can give.
>
> Changes only you can bring about.
>
> Causes only you can influence.

It is a perfect plan by a perfect Creator.

Pursue it with all your strength and you will be fulfilled.

"For I know the plans I have for you," declares the Lord, *"plans to prosper you and not to harm you, plans to give you hope and a future"* (Jeremiah 29:11).

God's unique plan for us will prosper us rather than harm us and will build hope and a significant future for our lives. The pursuit of His plan will allow us to be instruments of unique gifts, significant change, and productive influence. The pursuit of His plan will change the lives of those around us for the better and will bring us fulfillment.

There is a path for you to walk.

> Places only you can go.

> Hills that only you can climb.

> Bridges only you can cross.

> Treasures only you can find.

Take the high road and ignore the short cuts.

Enjoy the journey and always rely on the Lord as your guide.

After all, He is the one that made the pathway.

"The path of the righteous is like the morning sun, shining ever brighter till the full light of day." (Proverbs 4:18).

I promise you that the longer we follow God's path for our life, the clearer we see His hand on us. How do we stay on His path? We follow the light. When things get dimmer, we should examine our proximity to God's path for us and ask, "Is our love still strong? Are we living justly? Do we love mercy? Are we walking humbly? Follow the path that grows brighter, not dimmer.

There is a purpose for which you live.

Dreams only you can make come true.

People only you can love.

Children only you can raise.

Promises only you can keep.

You have caught God's eye and curried His favor.

You live in the shelter of His grace and

Succeed through the power of His purpose.

"Many are the plans in a person's heart, but it is the LORD'S PURPOSE THAT PREVAILS." (Proverbs 19:21).

Our purpose is to be a part of God's purpose. We are unique and our lives are important to Him. This uniqueness does not mean we are necessary, but we are important and we can be useful. We have caught God's eye and can be instruments of His grace, His mercy and His plan in a unique way. To accomplish this, we must always line up our plans with His purposes. Then we will succeed through the power of His purpose.

Thanks, Philip, for allowing me to share this.

Song to Consider: "Fearfully" – Charlie Hines

Prayer: Lord Jesus, You are always right. Your plans are perfect. Your ways are good. Your pathway gets brighter every passing day. I thank You that You have chosen me as one of Your dearly loved children. I can delight in the fact that I am important to You. May I honor You each day by remembering and acting on the fact that You have a plan, a path and a purpose for me that will bring me success, joy and fulfillment. Remind me every day that You have written all my days and that I am fearfully and wonderfully made for Your sake, Amen.

Promise and Possibility

As I write today, the weather in Cincinnati has improved, and temperatures are higher with some sunshine. The promise of springtime is rising inside of me. The past few days I have found myself humming or even singing the Gaither song, "I Am a Promise." Yes, the one of Veggie Tales fame. This simple song proclaims: _"I am a promise; I am a possibility. I am a promise with a capital 'P'; I am a great big bundle of potentiality."_ The song reminds me that the reason God, particularly in His work through Jesus, has always been able to capture the hearts of so many people is that He always sees promise and potential in every one of us. Down through the ages, God has been about the business of selecting people with promise and potential based on the knowledge that He has the power to work in them and through them to bring out hidden qualities. Potential that could meet needs, rally faithfulness, change cultures, and, yes, change the whole world. Let's recall a few of these stories.

Joseph was the youngest of his siblings, and we have reason to suspect that he had an arrogant streak that did not set well with his brothers. God allowed him to pass through a long training process that humbled him and taught him respect for authority and the truth. Because he learned his lesson well, he served the pagan Pharaoh with truthfulness and faithfulness resulting in the whole of Egypt, Israel and the surrounding world being saved from starvation. God saw the potential in Joseph that his jealous brothers never realized. He rose to be, arguably, the most powerful instrument of promise in the known world.

God told Samuel to journey away from Saul's inner circle of power and visit Jesse to look for a successor king. After inspecting all of Jesse's older sons, Samuel had them call the runt, David, in from the pasture to find God's choice for Israel's king. Jehovah saw promise and possibility in David that no one thought existed. As the song "Shepherd Boy" by Ray Boltz says, "When others see a shepherd boy, God may see a King."

Jesus, returning from His fast and temptation in the wilderness, saw some struggling fishermen in Galilee and challenged them. "Come with Me, and fish for people." Who could have ever realized that this uneducated group would overcome fear and persecution and change the history of the world with their powerful message of promise and possibility? Jesus saw the potential of faith in this group of men that would fight through hardship, disappointment and fear without losing the hope in the promise that Jesus was who He said He was and had indeed changed them.

Jesus saw the gift of evangelism in the woman He met at the well in Samaria. He looked through her shame and her sadness that others saw in her and knew she was searching for truth written in her heart rather than the scrolls in the temple. Immediately after her first taste of living water, she ran and brought the entire town to meet the living, breathing instrument of change in the earth.

How do we best follow Jesus? How do we best bring others to Jesus so He can change them like He has changed us? The simple truth is that we need to have His vision of promise, possibility and potential when we view others. It is so easy to see the warts, the flaws, the unseemly elements that plague all of the children of the flesh. We stereotype with the judgments -- they are too dirty, they are too sinful, they are too different for us to influence their lives. We discount the miracle-working power that has changed us, refusing to believe it is equally sufficient to change others; ignoring the truth that "to as many as receive Him, He gives the power to be the children of God." We refuse to take on possible rejection or confrontation when we know we have a mission to set aside our interests for the interests of God and His Kingdom's causes.

What if we could fight through our carnal mind's eyes and see with the eyes of our Creator? Wouldn't it be exhilarating to see the promise, possibility and potential in everyone we live with and live around every day? The wisdom of the world says, "Everyone for themselves," or "Invest in the ones most like me," and the spirit of destruction seeks to divide and conquer. The wisdom of our Father and our Lord says, "Whoever wants a drink of real life, drink freely," and "If I am lifted up, I will draw everyone to Me." The Spirit of Heaven works through men to gather together a family for the King of Heaven. His vision sees the promise, possibility and potential in every person because the good news (gospel) of Jesus is the power of God to save the best and the worst among us. Here's looking at you! Here's to seeing the promise, possibilities and potential in every one of you. You are special; you are the chosen! Let's go out and find some more special folks! They surround us.

When was the last time you reached out to someone, not at all like you, with kindness, compassion, grace, or good news? When was the last time you made a conscious effort to be the instrument to unlock potential in someone with whom you live, work and serve?

Song to Consider: "I Am a Promise" – Bill and Gloria Gaither

Prayer: Thank You, Father, that You looked beyond my fault and saw my needs. Thank You that You looked through my weaknesses, through my fears, through my self-centeredness, and recognized the promise and potential gathered for Your purposes and Your Kingdom's cause. Help me set aside my carnal eyes and choose to look at everyone around me with Your vision that recognizes promise, possibility and potential so that I can be encouraged to be a living, breathing instrument of positive change in the earth. For Jesus' sake, Amen.

The Good News of Grace

I have small business cards that I leave with those who provide me with excellent service. On the front of the card, it reads: "There is a seed of God in every heart that cannot grow unless it's watered by His grace." The back of the card reads: "May the grace of the Father of my Lord Jesus fall like gentle rain on your heart today." The reference is Hebrews 4:16, "Let us then approach God's throne of grace with confidence, so that we may receive mercy and *find grace to help us in our time of need*" (emphasis added).

I cannot fathom a life lived without grace, but I lived a large part of my life without fully understanding the mighty force of the good news of grace. I was in my fifties before the reality of the grace, visited on me throughout my life, came crashing down with all its fullness. I wept for days at the mere thought of how God's grace had come to me in such great measure and how grace sustained me without fail through every turn (right or wrong) of life. Years later, I can hardly converse with God or man about this grace very long without tears of great joy beginning to flow. The power of a great affection – the power of grace -- has seized me.

You see, God's gift of grace is more than unmerited favor; it is the power for us to do the things we should do. This power is far more than power over sin. Jesus solved the dilemma of our inability to keep the Law on the cross. He made us righteous (right with God), not necessarily perfect, at least not yet. This grace is consistently perfected within us by the life of God's Holy Spirit and is much more about the things we can do than the things we should not do. This *GOSPEL* changes lives. This Good News is more than an insurance policy for hell's fire; it is the power of righteousness, joy and peace in the Holy Spirit. This power translates into us being able to live right with a grateful heart that is content with what God has done and is doing in us, for us and through us.

"May our Lord Jesus Christ himself and God our Father, *who loved us and by his grace gave us eternal encouragement and good hope,* encourage your hearts and strengthen you in every good deed and word" (2 Thessalonians 2:16-17 emphasis added).

What is the good message of grace that works in us? It best answers these questions: Why am I hopeful? Why am I joyful? Why am I confident? Why am I kind? Why am I generous? Why am I patient? Everyone needs the answers to these questions. Grace brings answers to these questions. *We have been made right with God!* He made us right when we could not and would not get right. We have abundant life. This is the gospel and this is the good news. Grace changes lives from desperation to determination, from desolation to dedication, and from degradation to invaluable worth. It's the power to do what we ought to do. The power that is greater than all our sins. It's the power that transforms uselessness into usefulness.

God's grace is best served and not reserved. "Each of you should *use whatever gift you have received to serve others, as faithful stewards of God's grace in its various forms*" (1 Peter 4:10 emphasis added). Since God's grace is served to us by His Spirit, it takes the form of the Spirit's fruit -- hope, joy, faith, kindness, generosity, and patience. Once received, grace is most powerful when it's passed on to others. There is nothing like serving up the good news of grace. Its aroma is like home cooking, like serving southern sweet tea to thirsty folks or breaking out grandma's cinnamon rolls for breakfast. Grace is so, so good and satisfying; it leaves those served saying, "May I have some more, please." Then we can answer, "Taste and see that the Lord (and His grace) is good."

Do me a favor. Sit down, relax and enjoy a good helping of God's grace today. It's so very good. Savor it - it may even make you cry for joy. Then find someone to whom you can serve some also.

Song for Consideration: "Great Grace" – Mary Alessi

Prayer: Gracious Lord, work in me Your great grace through the power to fulfill my purposes, which You established before the world began. I have seen, on every hand, Your unmerited favor at every turn of life. You are faithful to compound the good and redeem the not so good that I have invested. Continue to perfect this work in me and through me for the praise of Your glory and Your Kingdom's eternal cause. You and Your amazing grace are so very, very good. Keep me, and those I touch, always coming back for more. For Jesus' sake, Amen.

Who Am I?

Just Who Do You Think You Are?

We have all heard the stories of people filled with pride that never get into the Kingdom of Heaven. Instances warning about pride and haughtiness fill up the Scriptures. Indeed, we are admonished to "Humble ourselves in the sight of the Lord and He will lift us up." But consider this, what if the exact opposite of pride is as dangerous to our relationship with God and His kingdom? What if we are so demeaning of ourselves, our worth and our lives that we miss the opportunity to participate fully in the blessings of the Kingdom of God? I have shared how there are great promise and possibilities in each of us, and that God always sees that promise and possibility when He looks at us, regardless of our current condition. Sometimes we fail to remember God's point of view, and we sell ourselves short.

My friend, Ron Wyrtzen, shared with our men's group a very acute observation about how we perceive who we are. He stated that when we demean ourselves, when we put ourselves down and hold ourselves in low esteem, we exhibit a high state of arrogance because we consider our opinion of who we are above God's opinion of who we are. If we doubt our purpose or our significance, we have no faith to believe that what God says about us is true. We leave our minds and hearts open to the great lie that the devil wants to perpetuate in all mankind. The lie that says you are worthless, you are of no significance and your life is meaningless to others and to God. I want us to review what God thinks about us and consider the question: *Who do we think we are?*

The Apostle John certainly knew who he was. He states in John 1, "…to all who did receive him, to those who believed in his name, he gave the right to become *children of God*— children born not of natural descent, nor of human decision or a husband's will, but born of God." In I John 3:1, he declares, "See what great love the Father has lavished on us, that we should be called *children of God!* And that is what we are!" We are God's children, His heirs, supernaturally adopted into His family. We are the children of the King of all creation, the family of the Giver of life, and purpose and meaning. We are not insignificant. The Treasure of Heaven has paid for all of us. To believe otherwise is a willful rejection of what God's Word and God's actions declare to us.

King David understood how God felt about him and who he was in God's eyes. With grateful praise he declared in Psalm 139, "I praise you because *I am fearfully and wonderfully made;* Your works [of which I am one] are wonderful, *I know that full well."* David had grasped the truth that I have spoken to you about before. He was unique and created to fulfill things no one else could do. He had a purpose given to him by the Creator. And we do too!

The Apostle Paul perceived the wonderful reality of God's purpose in choosing us for His family. Paul declares in Ephesians 1, *"In him we were also chosen,* having been predestined according to the plan of him who works out everything in conformity with the purpose of his will, *in order that we,* who were the first to put our hope in Christ, *might be for the praise of his glory."* We are chosen to bring God glory. More than the rest of God's creation, man can reflect God's glory because He created us in His likeness. We have the ability to look like God. We have the ability to be a temple in which His Spirit resides. Nothing else in creation can match this ability He put in us.

The Apostle Peter was confident in God's perception of us when he wrote in I Peter 2:9 "… you are a *chosen people,* a royal priesthood, a holy nation, *God's special possession,* that you may declare the praises of him who called you out of darkness into his wonderful light." He knew we are special to God. Paul knew we are chosen to declare the majesty and glory of the Lord of Creation by the way we live, talk, trust, and love.

We have a choice to believe as these great men of faith believed. We can believe that we are a treasure, the objects of God's divine affection, the fulfillment of His purpose in the earth, the heirs to abundant and everlasting life. Conversely, we can choose to accept the lie that we are insignificant, that we can only fail, that we lack in our ability to succeed in things that matter to God.

Let's decide to believe what God says about us. Let's live with purpose and significance every day. We can be a blessing to someone every day we live and bring a smile to Father's face. We carry the Spirit of the Lord of Creation and His Son inside of us. *Act as if we are the chosen; think of ourselves as God's dearly loved children and leave the lies behind.* Now, who do you think you are?

Song to Consider: "Hello, My Name Is" – Matthew West

Prayer: Father, I am Yours. You know how to care for what belongs to You. Forgive me when I forget who I am in You. Forgive me when my thoughts about myself deny what Your Word says about me. Come live in me and make me look more like You every day. I will no longer think of myself as insignificant, incapable, unworthy, and unloved. I choose to believe that I am one of Your chosen, fearfully and wonderfully made, that I am precious and that above all, You are faithful to complete Your plans and purposes in and through me every minute of every day as I choose to believe You, follow You and obey You, Amen.

God's Purpose for Us

> *Christianity started in Palestine as a fellowship;*
> *it moved to Greece and became a philosophy;*
> *it moved to Italy and became an institution;*
> *it moved to Europe and became a culture; it came*
> *to America and became an enterprise.*
>
> — *Sam Pascoe*

This concise history of Christianity reveals to us the desperate state of Christianity in the American culture. I am heartbroken when I consider my part in this. If the Church is Christ's body and we have actively participated in reducing it to a business, we have made the body of Christ like a prostitute. We have created a theology to soothe our conscience and get what we need. Tragically, the American Church, is heavily populated by people who do not love God. How can we love Him? We don't even know Him, and I mean *really* know Him. We have, in our unmitigated pride, shaped God's Kingdom into our own Americanism terms. Either we have to become exceptional and driven to know God and worship Him, or we choose to believe that we are simply good enough because we are, after all, Americans, and can gain His Kingdom with little or no change. This American Gospel is why money grubbers, pedophiles, sexual deviants, and social deviants who live in open defiance to God's laws populate the leadership of many American churches. This term Christian, in America, has become so distorted. Everyone lays claim to it, strives for it, while ignoring the demand for repentance and change.

I have long ago lost any passion for any enterprise that establishes rules we cannot keep and gives us jobs we cannot perform to gain God's favor. I have also painfully come to realize that, while a personal relationship with Jesus is free for the asking, following Him will require us to undergo the pain of change and may well cost us everything. How do we live like children of God, followers of Jesus? What is it that makes us peculiar, living lives in this world but not of this world? What is our hope? Let's try to understand God's purpose in choosing us to be His children.

Israel rejected Jesus because they could not understand the mission of His Kingdom. America, as well, fails to understand the mission of His Kingdom. We look for a sugar daddy, we look for Hell insurance, and we look for someone to paint over our sins rather than wash away our sins. We look for a Democrat Jesus to solve social injustices or a Republican, white, Anglo-Saxon Jesus to abolish murderers, homosexuals, drug addicts, and gamblers. Who is this Jesus? Why did He come for us? Why does He interrupt life and bother us? What is His ultimate motive?

Christ is not a creed, culture or an enterprise. Jesus is God, come in the flesh, revealed in a manner we can, at least, have a chance of comprehending. Christianity is a relationship. It is life itself because Jesus is life. At the beginning when God said to Jesus and the Holy Spirit, "Let us make man in Our image," He was motivated by love. He wanted to create something that could look like Him and love like Him. He desired an object for His divine affection. Thus, He made Adam, and then He made Eve. Divine love required giving men a choice whether to love in return. Adam and Eve chose to love themselves more than they loved God. Sin (rebellion) entered the world separating man from God, and God set His mind to resolving the problem of sin's separation in a permanent way. He did this by sending Christ to pay the price justice demanded and to restore man into the same manner of fellowship with God that God initially established in Eden.

The rebellion in Adam has been passed on to every person born. The rebellion in Adam brought a curse upon the creation God intended to be a garden of love for man and God. We sin by nature; we sin by choice; and we can't help it. On our own, we can't become good enough to satisfy the justice a perfect God requires. We can't through sacrifice, work, worship or apology return to the relationship of Eden. *We cannot change; someone must change us.* Being changed requires faith, repentance, and acceptance. These things we can do. John proclaimed, "to as many as received Him [Jesus], he gave the power to become children of God" (John 1:12).

God solved our sin problem through Christ who "became sin when He knew no sin so that we could become His righteousness" (II Corinthians

5:21). He exchanged His life for our life. We became His righteousness (people in right standing with God), not our righteousness.

Can we, once and for all, come to realize that Jesus did not die to make us perfect; He did not die to create worker bees; He did not die just to give us eternal life or just to keep us from going to hell. *He died to make us His, to make us, once again, the objects of His and His Father's divine affection,* restored to abundant, eternal, everlasting fellowship with the Creator of all things. God, the Father, exchanged a perfect life for imperfect lives, and this is all we need to know. We give Him our life in exchange for His life. He does not want what we can do; He does not want what we have; He just wants us. He wants us to be loved by Him and to return this love with our love. He wants us to know Him through experience, not just to know about Him. He wants us to learn of Him by touching Him with our hearts as well as our minds. If this exchange requires all of us for all of Him, then who gets the better end of the exchange? The 20th century martyr, Jim Elliot, exclaimed: "He is no fool who gives what he cannot keep to gain that which he cannot lose." We cannot keep this life we live and any of its trappings, but we can exchange it for Jesus, who is life - abundant, full, free and everlasting!

Song to Consider: "Jesus Messiah" – Chris Tomlin

Prayer: Father, bring to my heart understanding of why You chose me. Jesus, help me exchange my life for Yours every day. Holy Spirit, give me the wisdom to know You in my heart and not just with my mind. All that I have, all that I am, all that I hope to be, I give to You in exchange for all You gave for me and to understand that all of me is what You want and what You have always wanted. Amen

Fit for a King

My friend, Ron, related a story that the pastor of his church showed up one Sunday morning wearing a baseball cap. He proceeded to greet people at the door and continued to wear the cap through the worship service and even while he delivered his Sunday message. The following week he returned to address the congregation about the baseball cap situation, as he had (not unexpectedly) received much telephone and email input regarding the wearing of the cap. His statement to the congregation was profound. He told them, "Many of you provided much input about whether it was proper to wear a baseball cap in the Lord's house last week. I challenge your premise that I wore a cap in the Lord's house. You see, I contend that *I wore a cap on the Lord's house.*" God's house is not brick and mortar or wood and paint; God's house is flesh, blood, and spirit and He desires it to be a place made fit for a king.

The Apostle Paul, while addressing the problem of sexual misconduct in the church at Corinth writes, "Don't you realize that *your body is the temple of the Holy Spirit, who lives in you and was given to you by God? You do not belong to yourself,* for God bought you with a high price. *So you must honor God with your body*" (I Cor. 6:19-20 emphasis added). Honoring God with our bodies goes far beyond refraining from sexual misconduct. It encompasses all aspects of how we care for our mind, our spirit and our body. We must be willing to cooperate with God's Spirit as He takes us through the process of redecorating His home. We must be willing to refrain from taking into our eyes and ears and minds those things which are coarse and degrading that the world may think of as humorous and titillating. The books, magazines, TV shows, movies, and conversation that the world engages in can have a demeaning effect on the Master of our house. It should have a sobering effect on us. If we stifle God's Spirit by the condition we leave His house in, we will experience more turmoil and less peace in our inner being.

We also need to realize we must take care of our bodies so that they remain an effective and functional dwelling place. We must purpose to keep them clean, well rested, well nourished, and well exercised (ouch for me). If we are faithful in these matters, we will be effective instruments of peace, grace, hope, and service to all of those around us for many years.

The King of Creation has come to dwell in us, and when we invite Him in, He enters as a guest but desires to become Master of our house. We may initially make a concerted effort to tidy up the living room and guest room. As His stay in us lengthens, we find He begins to notice our messy basement, our hidden closets and our junk drawers, and He lovingly presses us to clean up every corner of His dwelling, discarding the junk and the trash. We may view ourselves as a framed hut, but Jesus desires a palace to dwell in. Our heart's desire should be to attend constantly to the state of His dwelling. After all, He will be staying a long, long time (forever).

Scripture:

I Corinthians Chapter 6

Psalm 84

Have you ever considered what a privilege it is to dwell with the presence of the Creator? That He has chosen to live in you?

Song to Consider: "How Lovely is Your Dwelling Place" - Matt Redman

Prayer: Thank You, my King, that You have come to dwell in me. Make me always attentive to Your desire to dwell in a place fit for Your glory. Strengthen me to open every door and every space of myself and allow You to direct my renovation. Help me to haul out the old junk and avoid bringing in things that might grieve You. May I become a palace of peace that others can easily see is a place where You dwell. For You alone are worthy to receive honor and glory both now and forever, Amen.

Good News for Crack(ed)pots

One of the greatest lies we can believe is that our messed up condition prohibits God from using us for His purposes. We sit back nursing our perceived wounds of incompetence, holding our soiled laundry, trying to hide our defects, waiting for God to correct all these flaws so we can be of some use to Him.

So often the shame of our past taunts us and leaves us immobilized by fear and self-hatred. But there's a better way. God's gift to us is one of redemption, grace and forgiveness. It's a love predicated on using everything for His glory, despite how tragically flawed or defective we may feel about ourselves or past actions or events.

No matter how worthless, unloved or unwanted we may feel, God still wants to use us. No matter how troubled our past or challenged our present, He has made us be His instruments of peace, grace, mercy, and yes, His pleasure. *Our LORD has the power to use us even as He engages in the process of changing us.* His care loses nothing to the process.

The Apostle Paul reminded the Corinthians that, when he pleaded with God to remove a particular defect in him, God said, " *'My power shows up best in weak people.'* Now I am glad to boast about how weak I am; I am glad to be a living demonstration of Christ's power, instead of showing off my own power and abilities. Since I know it is all for Christ's good, I am quite happy about "the thorn," and about insults and hardships, persecutions and difficulties; for when I am weak, then I am strong—*the less I have, the more I depend on him*" (2 Corinthians 12:9-10 TLB).

In his book *Ruthless Trust,* Brennan Manning shared this Buddhist parable known as, "The Legend of the Cracked Pot" that aptly describes how God can use the mess in our lives and transform us into something beautiful.

> *A water bearer in India had two large pots; one hung on each end of a pole which he carried across his neck and shoulders. One of the pots had a crack in it, and while the other pot was perfect and always delivered a full portion of water at the end of the long walk*

from the stream to the master's house, the cracked pot arrived only half full.

For two years this was the daily routine, with the water bearer delivering only one and a half pots full of water to his master's house. Of course, the perfect pot was proud of its accomplishments, performing perfectly as purposed. On the other hand, the cracked pot was ashamed of its imperfections and felt itself a failure since it was only capable of accomplishing half the task it had been made to do. The bitterness grew, and the cracked pot finally found the courage to speak to the bearer. "I am ashamed of myself, and I want to apologize to you."

"Why?" asked the bearer. "What are you ashamed of?"

"I have failed to fulfill the purpose I was made for. I am only capable of delivering half the water because of the crack in my side. You have to do all this work, and you do not get full value for your efforts," the pot said.

*The water bearer said to the pot, "Have you noticed the flowers that grow alongside the path? They are there because I planted seeds, knowing that as we walked back up the path, your dripping water would nourish them. I have been able to provide flowers for the master's table because of the water that you provided the flowers. **Without you being just the way you are, there would have been no time to grow the flowers. You have not failed; your flaws produced something beautiful"** (Manning 133-135).*

The process of our change will take a lifetime. Let's fall into the Master's arms of grace and mercy now so He uses us every day according to His divine purposes. He takes great pleasure in using the improbable to work the impossible – changing out the beauty of His power for the ashes of our weakness and exchanging our wretched rags for the riches of His glorious cause. Rise, all you who are downhearted! God knows the best way to convince sinners of His mercy is to send them sinners who they know are being changed to share the good news. Take heart, all you cracked pots. He will find a use for you today.

Song to Consider: "I Will Rise" – Shawn McDonald

Prayer: Father, no matter how imperfect I feel, I trust You to make me new. I look forward, in faith to my perfection, and in the meantime, give myself, the good and the not so good, for Your use and Your purposes in the world around me. Make Yourself strong in my weakness and profound in my simplicity. **Use me and my cracks to water seeds of grace and mercy in everyone I touch** as You continue to change me into all You have purposed for me to be. In Jesus' name, Amen.

Take heart; it is the Father's pleasure to give you the Kingdom.

Who Is God?

Be Still

Brother Lawrence, famous for his ability to practice the presence of God, related, "That there needed neither art nor science for going to God, but _only a heart resolutely determined to apply itself to nothing but Him,_ of for His sake, and to love Him only." Brother Lawrence believed we were created to love God and nothing else and that all other things in life flowed from the love of God.

I have been reading Colossians and I am focused on the second chapter where Paul gives a blueprint for a godly life. Colossians 2:9-12 reads, "For this reason, since the day we heard about you, we have not stopped praying for you. We continually ask _God to fill you with the knowledge_ of his will through all the wisdom and understanding that the Spirit gives, so that you may live a life worthy of the Lord and please him in every way: bearing fruit in every good work, growing in the knowledge of God, being strengthened with all power according to his glorious might so that you may have great endurance and patience, and giving joyful thanks to the Father, who has qualified you to share in the inheritance of his holy people in the kingdom of light" (emphasis added).

So what is the knowledge of God and His will? We must become still and experience His presence, His love, His voice, His heart. I want to share with you the word of the Lord as told to me just before dawn on a glorious spring day... He whispered,

"Come to Me all you who carry a heavy burden and I will give you rest.

BE STILL – and know that I Am God.
Bigger than all of creation,
The Light that pierces the darkness,

The air you breathe,
The sun that warms you,
The rain that sustains you,
The bread that feeds you.

BE STILL – and know that I Am holy.
Perfect in all My ways,
Righteous in all My judgments,
The foundation of all wisdom,
Intentional in all my acts,
I do not, have not, and will not fail.

BE STILL – and know that I Am lovely.
I am present in the sunrise,
In the glory of a rose,
In the kindness of a stranger,
In the beauty of a snow-covered meadow,
In the warmth of a winter's fire.

BE STILL – and know My name is mercy.
I have chosen you.
Know how far I came to find you.
All I paid to redeem you.
The grace it takes to keep you,
The power of My affection,
The focus of My perfect desire.

BE STILL – and know that I Am eternal.
I am present now, always have been, always will be,
I am timeless, swallowing the ages,
Blinking at light years while holding
The ever-expanding universe in My fingers.

BE STILL – and know that I Am faithful.
My promises are true.
I finish all I begin,
Holding all I have created in its place.
I hold on to you – even when you can't hold on to Me.

BE STILL – and know that you are Mine.
Chosen from the beginning,
Born of My spirit,
Adopted by My will,
Kept by My covenant,
Resting in My unfailing love.

BE STILL… and know… I AM.

When was the last time you were totally still before God? No sound, no distractions, no anxious thoughts? How did it feel? Isn't it worth trying to return to that place?

He is glorious. He is eternal. He is everywhere. He is with us, around, in us, and over us. Like the air we breathe, unseen yet sustaining life. Let's do more practicing the presence of God every day. He is great, He is kind, and He is good all the time.

Song to Consider: "Glorious" - Paul Baloche

Prayer: Jesus, there is none like You. Show me Your glory every day in new ways. Give me eyes to see the glory of the Lord. Help me take the time to be still and practice Your presence. You fill up the universe. You fill up my heart and bring joy to my soul, Amen.

The Voice of the Lord

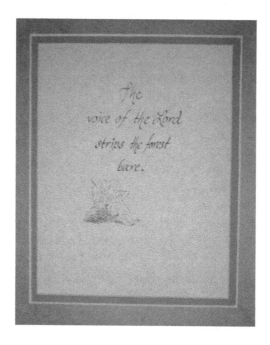

A simple framed yet beautiful paraphrased drawing of Psalm 29:9 hangs on the wall of our den. The pen and ink piece was produced and given to us by my talented and artistic nephew, David. It has been hanging in our den well over fifteen years. Like other pieces in our house, it so often gets lost in its familiarity to the surroundings. Lately, I have been drawn to its simple beauty and powerful message. To someone with a prophetic gift, hearing and understanding the voice of the Lord becomes a yearning of the heart. God's voice and words are important to our wellbeing and our direction. To those of us with a prophetic gift, it is urgent that we know His voice, hear Him clearly, understand His words, and faithfully pass them on because there are others depending on our faithfulness to our calling. This calling is what my devotions are for; to pass on to my family what God is speaking to my heart. However, the truth is that any of us can hear His voice because He lives in us. He is faithful to speak instruction to all of us who He dwells in if we will earnestly listen and then obey what we hear. It is important for all of us to recognize God's voice, understand what He says, and then actively obey His instruction. So, what is the voice of God and how do we know it? Let's look at some scriptures that will lead us down the pathway to a greater understanding of "the voice of the Lord."

> "The voice of the Lord is over the waters; the God of glory thunders, the Lord thunders over the mighty waters. The voice of the LORD is powerful; the voice of the LORD is majestic. The voice of the LORD breaks the cedars; the LORD breaks in pieces the cedars of Lebanon. He makes Lebanon leap like a calf, Sirion like a young wild ox. The voice of the LORD strikes with flashes of lightning. The voice of the LORD shakes the desert; the LORD shakes the Desert of Kadesh. The voice of the Lord twists the oaks and strips the forests bare" (Psalm 29:3-9).

First, the scriptures are full of references to the power of God's voice and His words. I believe that those of us who truly know Him can hear His voice in nature. He will reward those who diligently (intentionally) seek Him. Through the bird's song in the early morning God declares, "I Am the great I Am, wondrous are My ways, glorious is the life I create, I am mindful of the sparrow and much more mindful of you." He speaks through nature, "I Am lovely, I Am present in the sunrise, in the glory of a rose, in the beauty of a snow-covered meadow and the warmth of a winter fire." I have heard His voice in the music of the ocean's tide on the east coast of America reciting, "I Am faithful, never changing, and great in mercy, good all the time." When is the last time we came to a place of rest and heard the voice of God in His creation around us? David knew His voice in nature and faithfully declared it to those around him. Let everyone who has an ear listen and hear the voice of the Lord!

Another thing I believe that David realized is the power of God's voice is not in its decibels or in its ability to be determined by the human ear. It is the power of tenderness, reason, truth, and stability that strips the forest bare and divides asunder the affairs of our hearts. God's voice has the power to light up the darkness, shout down lies, bring hope to the hopeless, and break down strongholds that bind people to despair with just a whisper of tenderness. Let everyone who has an ear listen and hear the voice of the Lord!

"Samuel was lying down in the house of the LORD, where the ark of God was. Then the LORD called Samuel. Samuel answered, "Here I am." And he ran to Eli and said, "Here I am; you called me."But Eli said, "I did not call; go back and lie down." So he went and lay down. Again the LORD called, "Samuel!" And Samuel got up and went to Eli and said, "Here I am; you called me.""My son," Eli said, "I did not call; go back and lie down." *Now Samuel did not yet know the* Lord: *The word of the LORD had not yet revealed to him.* A third time the LORD called, "Samuel!" And Samuel got up and went to Eli and said, "Here I am; you called me." *Then Eli realized that the LORD was calling the boy. So Eli told Samuel, "Go and lie down, and if he calls you, say, 'Speak, Lord, for your servant is listening.'"* So Samuel went and lay down in his place. The LORD came and stood there, calling as at the other times, "Samuel! Samuel!" *Then Samuel said, "Speak, for your servant is listening." And the LORD spoke to Samuel for the rest of his life"* (I Samuel 3:3-11 emphasis added).

The Lord will only speak to those who acknowledge that they are listening. Jesus was the most intentional person who ever lived. He never wasted breath, much less a word. God will not speak to hear Himself talk. He speaks with purpose to those who are open to His voice and willing to obey. Samuel had not yet learned God's voice. He only heard Him speak after He acknowledged he was listening. From that time forward, Samuel heard a lot from God, and he faithfully communicated the Word of God to the kings and the people of Israel. The more we acknowledge to God we are listening, the more He will communicate to our spirits. Eventually, we can achieve a constant dialog with the One who lends us significance and purpose and everlasting life. Unlike Samuel in the beginning, the living Word of God, Jesus, lives in us and reveals Himself and His words to us. But, like Samuel, we need to acknowledge to Him that we are listening and willing to obey.

We also have the written word of God to direct and instruct us. This written word is most definitely the voice of God, and its proclamation is powerful and sharper than a sword to expose the affairs and intent of the deceitful human heart. We must remember that the discerned voice of the Lord we hear in our spirit (inner ear) will never instruct or direct in conflict with His written word, to which we have, thankfully, continual access. How much time do we spend reading and studying the written word of the Lord? The understanding of the contents in His written word opens up our spirit to much more personal and practical instruction by the voice we hear in our "inner ear"." The diligent study of His written word becomes our response, "Speak, for your servant is listening." We live in the information age, and there are thousands of voices speaking at the same time vying for our attention. Magazines, blogs, books, and movies consume much of our attention and speak information which is, many times, contrary to the voice of the Lord. Hear me when I tell you: study the written word of God! It is powerful, and a little bit will go a long way to countermand the other, less godly voices we are hearing. If we will set aside ten minutes a day to study God's written word two things will happen. First, we will soon find out that ten minutes is not enough, and secondly, we will long for more of His word and find out that we will begin to hear the voice of the Lord more clearly with our (inner ear) spirit. Let everyone who has an ear listen and hear the voice of the Lord!

Song to Consider: "The Voice of the Lord" – Philips, Craig and Dean

Prayer: Father, I am so grateful that Your Living Word dwells in my heart. I incline my ear toward You. Speak, for Your servant is listening. I will intentionally draw near and listen to You speak to my inner ear. Give me strength to intentionally study Your written word so You can, with great power, instruct me how and when to obey You. I wait, with great anticipation, to hear You call my name so I can respond, "Speak Lord, for your servant is listening." For Jesus' sake, Amen.

The Eyes of the Lord

I am told I have my father's eyes. Many times I've heard some of you say, "You look like your father, especially your eyes." My sister has my father's eyes. Although she bears a striking resemblance to my mom, she has the familiar brown eyes of my dad. We are his children and so it naturally follows that we would look like him. This resemblance is a good thing. He's a good looking guy!

If we are children of God, we should bear some resemblance to Him. I hope that when others see our eyes, they are reminded of the compassionate and tender eyes of Jesus. Additionally, if we have our Heavenly Father's eyes, we should be able to see from His point of view. Though we can never see all things like Father does, we are well off when we can see things from His point of view. Let me tell you four things about the eyes of the Lord and His point of view.

First, the eyes of the Lord see everything in full detail. He is attentive to all the affairs of man and all we do. Hebrews 4:13 tells us, "Nothing in all creation is hidden from God's sight. Everything is uncovered and laid bare before the eyes of him to whom we must give account." Psalm 33:13-14 says, "From heaven the Lord looks down and sees all mankind; from his dwelling place he watches all who live on earth." We must be mindful that His attention is all encompassing, but it is also very personal. We are mistaken if we think He is so busy watching everything we can escape His examination. Proverbs 5:21 reminds us, "For your ways are in full view of the Lord, and he examines all your paths."

While we do not have Father's ability to see all things in detail, I do believe He calls us to be more attentive to what is around us. Whether it is raising our children, attending to the needy, encouraging the discouraged, confronting wrongdoing in a loving way, He asks us to up our game and do a better job being more attentive and responsive than those who do not share His point of view. I have had to repent for missing opportunities to do all of the above simply because my view was not as attentive as God would have it be. My distraction or busyness trumped attentiveness to sacred things.

We need to understand that humility attracts God's attention. He focuses His gaze on the humble and the lowly of heart. Psalm 138:6 says, "Though the Lord is exalted, he looks kindly on the lowly; though [he is] lofty, he sees them from afar." A humble spirit is attractive to God and invites His attention while the scriptures remind us that He [God] resists the proud. The plight of the needy draws His attention. In Mark 6 we are told, "Jesus landed and saw a large crowd, he had compassion on them, because they were like sheep without a shepherd. So he began to teach them many things."

If we have God's viewpoint, the lowly will not escape our view, and we will see opportunities to show compassion to them and to tell them the good news [gospel] that is at work changing our lives and growing hope in our hearts.

The Father turns His eyes to people with great faith. Matthew 9:1-2 tells us the story about a paralyzed man brought on a mat to Jesus by several of his friends. "When Jesus saw their faith, he said to the man, 'Take heart, son; your sins are forgiven.'" When the religious crowd took exception to His ability to forgive sins, Jesus said, "OK, since you think it is harder to heal him than to forgive him, I will go ahead and heal him." The man immediately got up and walked away healed. Later, in this same chapter, a woman sick for many years, simply reached out and touched Jesus' garment and was healed. When Jesus looked at this woman, He replied, "Your faith has healed you."

Are we drawn to great faith? Can we recognize when people are willing to believe God? Are we looking for these people? We must, as followers of Christ, expand our attention to include an attraction to people willing to believe what Jesus has to say and seize the opportunity to share Father's Good News of life-changing power.

God's eyes are attentive to those who are willing to follow after Him. In Matthew 4: 18-19 we are told, "As Jesus was walking beside the Sea of Galilee, *he saw* two brothers, Simon called Peter, and his brother Andrew. They were casting a net into the lake, for they were fishermen. 'Come, follow me,' Jesus said, 'and I will send you out to fish for people.'" These fellows immediately left their nets and followed Jesus. 2 Chronicles 16:9 says, "For the eyes of the Lord range throughout the earth to strengthen those whose hearts are fully committed to Him." We have been chosen to follow Christ, and His eyes are on us to strengthen us as we walk with Him and learn His ways and come to share His heart.

The last point I want to make about Father's eyes is that **they fix on the righteous.** Psalm 34:15-16 reminds us, "The eyes of the Lord are on the righteous and his ears attentive to their cry." Genesis 6:8-9 states that while God was angry with the sinfulness of mankind, "… *Noah found favor in the eyes* of the Lord…. Noah was a righteous man, blameless among the people of his time, and he walked faithfully with God." I want us to understand that righteous does not mean perfect. Although we are capable of error, *we have been made righteous and blameless through faith in Jesus Christ* (Romans 3). Our Father's eyes are fixed on us because we have been made righteous in His sight.

I want to keep my Father's eyes. I want to share His point of view. I want to see chances to change my world by giving attention to the opportunities to be an instrument of His grace, mercy, love, peace, and righteousness. The Father's eyes focus on us, and He calls out, "Do you see what I see?" Let's have eyes that resemble Jesus' eyes in how they look and what they see.

Song: "My Father's Eyes" – Amy Grant

Prayer: Father, thank You that You are changing the way I look and the way I see. Give me Your vision so that I can see the eternal things that are more valuable than earthly treasures. Give me Your vision that I can see an opportunity to change my world for the sake of Your kingdom's cause. Give me Your vision so that I can be attentive to the work of Your Spirit calling people to You and building faith in their hearts. In Jesus' name, Amen.

The Face of God

CNN called it "the embrace that melted hearts worldwide" as Pope Francis caught the attention of the world when he embraced and blessed a severely disfigured man at the Vatican.

This act of compassion reminded me about our responsibility to see Jesus in everyone. It is easy to love those who love us back, to love those who are lovely, to bless those who bless us, to help those who can help us. We live in a culture that worships physical beauty, worships success, worships the strong. That's the wisdom of the world. Let's think about what Jesus called us to.

> "Then Jesus said to his host, 'When you give a luncheon or dinner, do not invite your friends, your brothers or sisters, your relatives, or your rich neighbors; if you do, they may invite you back and so you will be repaid. *But when you give a banquet, invite the poor, the crippled, the lame, the blind, and you will be blessed. Although they cannot repay you, you will be repaid at the resurrection of the righteous*" (Luke 14:12-14 emphasis added).

> "When the Son of Man comes in his glory, and all the angels with him, he will sit on his glorious throne. All the nations will be gathered before him, and he will separate the people one from another as a shepherd separates the sheep from the goats. He will put the sheep on his right and the goats on his left. Then the King will say to those on his right, 'Come, you who are blessed by my Father; take your inheritance, the kingdom prepared for you since the creation of the world. For I was hungry, and you gave me something to eat, I was thirsty, and you gave me something to drink, I was a stranger, and you invited me in, I needed clothes, and you clothed me, I was sick, and you looked after me, I was in prison, and you came to visit me.' Then the righteous will answer him, 'Lord, when did we see you hungry and feed you, or thirsty and give you something to drink? When did we see you a stranger and invite you in or needing clothes and clothe you? When did we see you sick or in prison and go to visit you?' The King will reply, '*Truly I tell you, whatever you did for one of the least of these*

brothers and sisters of mine, you did for me." (Matthew 25:31-36 emphasis added).

We have a calling to let others see Jesus in us. We have a calling to see Jesus in others. Based on these two stories, Jesus tells us that we often find His face in the faces of the distressed, disfigured, downtrodden, poor, and powerless.

Where does our attention focus? Are we looking for the face of God in the right places? The bruises, scars and limps of the powerless are marks of God's ownership and, according to Matthew, His glory will be revealed in all of these on the Day of Judgment. We are the chosen of Christ, and we will never be able to dismiss the call to find Jesus in all men. Our lives will constantly be interrupted with inconvenient opportunities to embrace what the world abandons. We can count on it - Jesus is faithful to reveal Himself to those He calls His own.

Song to Consider: "Face of Christ" - Chris Rice

Prayer: Jesus, help me find Your face in new and different places today. Help me search for Your face with compassion, grace, mercy, and generosity. Give me a heart that longs to embrace You wherever You show up and hands to serve You wherever You demand. Amen.

There Can Be Only One

I remember today that there can be only one Savior. We dare not trust in anything or anyone but Jesus for our physical or eternal lives. All else and all others will fail us. It is easy for us to look to our parents, spouse, siblings, children, employers, or government for our needs. All of these can be instruments of provision, but provision and life emanate from only one source: the creative power of the Word of God (Jesus). We enter dangerous territory when we look apart from Him for our needs or when we try to fill His place in someone else's life.

God told Isaiah, "I am the Lord: that is My name: and My glory will I not give to another, neither My praise to graven images."

In Acts 4, Peter, filled with the Holy Spirit declared, "Salvation is found in no-one else, for there is no other name under heaven given to mankind by which we must be saved."

We all want friends and family on who we can depend. But when we see these people as our deliverance, when we look to them for solutions before we look to God, we become idol worshippers. We set ourselves up for great disappointment when we ascribe God's capabilities to humans regardless of how great their integrity and character may seem. Think about this in light of Mark 10:29-30, "'Truly I tell you,' Jesus replied, 'no one who has left home or brothers or sisters or mother or father or children or fields for me and the gospel will fail to receive a hundred times as much in this present age: homes, brothers, sisters, mothers, children and fields—along with persecutions—and in the age to come eternal life.'" Jesus demands elevation above all others as THE SOURCE. All grace, mercy, love, provision, and protection emanate from Him. He might choose to pass these things on through others, but He is always THE SOURCE. We must treat Him as divine and forsake all notions that others share in His divinity.

Furthermore, we all want to be useful to those we care for and to be instruments of grace and mercy. But when we represent ourselves as the ultimate solution to others' needs, facilitating their escape from every pain and care in the world, we elevate ourselves to a position of savior. Jesus alone reserves this place. We dare not assume or presume

His place. We are the vessels; He is the wine. We are the plate; He is the bread. The Savior's viewpoint is eternal and omniscient. Jesus has all the information to make decisions that will facilitate perseverance, hope, faith, and eternal life. Our viewpoint is temporal and incomplete, and we may choose to ease tribulation when tribulation is the required instrument of deliverance and growth. My father always said, "Don't feed people steak when God wants them on a bologna diet." Any attempts to ease trial and pain ordained by God's purposes stunt the growth of increased faith and dependence on God, whether it happens in our lives or the lives of others. Indeed, a life lived without need will result in eternal loss. We best meet the God of Salvation in the barren plains of desperate need.

Song to Consider: "Cornerstone" – Hillsong

My Song: Almighty God

I cannot help but bow before Your throne of awesome power.
I cannot help but fall into Your tender arms of love.
There is no other name for which all power and praise is worthy.
There is no other grace that reaches down to set me free.

You're the Almighty God, Ruler of creation;
A loving father with a home for all in need.
You're a mighty Savior, the Rock of our salvation.
A fountain of mercy, love and grace poured over me.

Pour over me, Oh Holy One,
For mercy's sake, come fill me up.
Til all I am brings glory to Your wondrous love,
And to Your name Almighty God;
I bring my praise Almighty God.

To You I gladly bring this song of humble adoration.
To You I offer up myself an instrument of praise.
There is no other shelter where my soul can run for refuge.
There is no other hand that reaches down to rescue me.

You're the Almighty God, ruler of creation;
A loving father with a home for all in need.
You're a mighty Savior, the rock of our salvation.
A fountain of mercy, love and grace poured over me.

Prayer: Lord Jesus, You alone are God of all. Your ways are true and everlasting. Your purposes are pure and eternal. You are THE SOURCE of all I need. Help me to look to You alone for salvation – both physically and spiritually. Keep me from trusting in idols -- even when they have kind and generous motives. Make me an instrument in Your hands: a glass full of Your Spirit; a plate for Your bread of life; a temple for Your dwelling. Not to us, Oh Lord, but to Your name be glory, and honor and praise. Amen.

Living with God

Living Close to God

I want to share with you some things that will let us practice living closer to God.

We were made to live in perfect and perpetual fellowship with our Creator. Unlike the rest of creation, man was intricately formed by God's hands, and then God kissed us with His breath and His life. Made in His image, Adam and Eve walked in intimate fellowship with God. Adam and Eve fell from this perfect way of living when they believed the lie that they could gain God's wisdom by disobeying God's command. They wanted God's place even though they already had God Himself. How foolish of them. The result of their sin (rebellion) made them ashamed, and they hid from God. They did not want Him to see them naked (which He was already able to do), and they did not want Him to know where they were (which He always knew). Their sin did not limit God; it stunted them and their ability to relate to God.

If we believe in Jesus and receive Him into our hearts, we receive the power to become God's children (John 1:12). What is the power that makes us God's children? The blood of Jesus is the power that makes us God's children. Sin separates us from God. It makes us ashamed and makes us want to hide. Jesus spilled out His blood to once and for all pay for our sin. We are made perfect in God's eyes when we believe in Jesus.

The Old Testament Law required the priest to enter into the Holy of Holies once a year and present a blood offering to cover his sins and the sins of the people they may have forgotten about throughout the year. This animal blood covered the altar; and God accepted it as covering for their sins. I urge you to read Hebrews 9. It is a wonderful explanation of the how Jesus, once and for all, changed this requirement.

Jesus' blood did not just cover sin; it washed sin away. No more would continual blood offerings be required to cover sins; the blood of Jesus provided a way for us to not just be covered, but to be clean. Not since Adam and Eve left the garden could sin be washed away. In God's eyes, those of us who receive Christ are washed clean. He perpetually sees us this way. When we sin now, we are the ones who suffer shame and we are the ones who run and hide. How do we return to a confident knowledge that God is close? How do we overcome our shame and come out of the bushes?

Three simple things allow us to live with the confidence of God's closeness. They are confession, repentance and obedience.

Confession acknowledges our condition. It is the action that says to God, "I am over here in the bushes sewing on my fig leaf. Can I return to your embrace?" To this God always responds, "Of course, My child. I know where you are and what you've done, and I still love you. It's all good." I John 1:9 states, "If we *confess our sins,* he is faithful and just and will *forgive us our sins and purify us* from all unrighteousness."

Repentance simply means to turn around and face God. It is hard to continue sinning when we remain face to face with God. Repentance acknowledges that we are not good at handling our affairs and that we realize our motives, outside of God's spirit, are harmful to us. Repentance is a change in the way we think and act. Regardless of how far away we think we have wandered from God, all we have to do is turn around, and He is there, face to face. Acts 26:20: "…I preached that they should repent and **turn to God** and demonstrate their **repentance** by their deeds."

Obedience is simply doing what Jesus does. Listen to what Micah says about obedience. "You have shown me what is good and what the Lord requires of me. That is to live justly, love mercy, and walk humbly with God." Jesus goes on to say that God's commands can be simply summed up as: "love the Lord with all our mind, heart and strength, and love others as much as we love ourselves" (Matthew 22:37-39). This command is the essence of obedience. "And this is love: that we walk in **obedience** to his commands. As you have heard from the beginning, his command is that you walk in love" (2 John 1:6).

Let's learn to practice confession, repentance and obedience every day so we can avoid spending our time in the bushes sewing on fig leaves. He more than covers our sins; He washes *our sin, our past, and our shame away*. Hiding from Father is not a necessary way of life for those who have received the power to be His dearly loved children.

Song to Consider: "Moving Forward" – Israel Houghton

My Song: Christ Is Here

Christ is here, come shout for joy,
He has overcome the darkness
By the glory of His face.
Prepare our hearts; worship and praise.
He's our promise of salvation,
Bringing hope and consolation,
Our sweet song of adoration hails His reign.
Christ is here.

Worthy is the Lamb;
The Lamb for sinners slain.
Risen and exalted Savior,
Lord of everything!

Christ is here, raise up your voice.
He has chased away our sorrows,
Given reason to rejoice.
Lift up our hands and bless His name.
His spirit lives in intercession,
He has covered our transgressions,
By His suffering and His wounds He heals our pain.
Christ is here.

Prayer: Father God, I will no longer hide in shame from You. I am here where You can see me and find me and gather me in Your loving arms. I confess Your way is best, I repent and turn to face You, and in obedience, I will follow You forward because You make all things new. In Jesus' precious name, Amen.

One Day at a Time

As I look back on sixty-plus years of my life and the twists and turns I have encountered along the way, I am amazed at where I am now. I am also a little disappointed at all the hours I have spent worrying about the future or fearfully pondering when the other shoe is going to drop. I can never dispute that life is hard at times and has its troubles, but I must say with the psalmist, "Surely goodness and mercies have followed me all the days of my life." I feel impressed to tell all of you, especially my children and grandchildren that, for all the plans we make and the worries we borrow, we can only live life one day at a time. Read the beautiful advice from Jesus from Matthew 6:25-34:

> "Therefore I tell you, _do not worry about your life_, what you will eat or drink; or about your body, what you will wear. _Is not life more than food, and the body more than clothes? Look at the birds of the air;_ they do not sow or reap or store away in barns, and yet your heavenly Father feeds them. _Are you not much more valuable than they?_ Can any one of you by worrying add a single hour to your life? And why do you worry about clothes? See how the flowers of the field grow. They do not labor or spin. Yet I tell you that not even Solomon in all his splendor was dressed like one of these. If that is how God clothes the grass of the field, which is here today and tomorrow is thrown into the fire, will he not much more clothe you—you of little faith? _So do not worry, saying, 'What shall we eat?' or 'What shall we drink?' or 'What shall we wear?' For the pagans run after all these things,_ and your heavenly Father knows that you need them. But seek first his kingdom and his righteousness, and all these things will be given to you as well. _Therefore do not worry about tomorrow, for tomorrow will worry about itself._ Each day has enough trouble of its own" (emphasis added).

I am not advocating a life without plans. I am advocating a life of planning around God's purpose for us. Remember what I said previously about God seeing us as a promise and a possibility? I am advocating a flexible attitude that bows before our Creator and our Lord with the knowledge that we belong to Him and that our view of life is limited while His view of life is eternal. This attitude is an attitude of faith.

If we borrow trouble, we deny God's goodness towards us. If we plan around calamity, we encourage a life of self-centeredness and stinginess that thwarts God's plan for us to contribute generosity and mercy and then reap it a hundred fold. Paul told the Romans, "The righteous will live by faith." The failure to live by faith puts us in a situation where we can excuse self-centered decisions and defend our right to govern our destiny.

Hebrews 11:6 tells us: *"Without faith it is impossible to please God."* Based on the end of Matthew 6, God has purposed that we should spend our energy on the decisions of today, making sure they are good ones. When I measure my scars at the age of 60, I realize that I have suffered the most from self-inflicted wounds made by bad decisions when I was not trusting God to direct my life. It was not the circumstances that battered me most, rather the poor choices I made without faith. My father has told me more than once, "We do not break God's commandments; we only break ourselves against them."

My final thoughts today are, regardless of how little faith we have exercised in the past, it only takes a mustard seed amount of faith to change us and to change our lives. We can get back on the path to God's purpose for us with a simple "Yes Lord" and a determination to make one good decision followed up by one more good decision. That first good decision is simply - Jesus I belong to You and I am going to follow Your lead and trust You to change me today. It does not matter how far we have come, we still need to be changed. The decision to follow Jesus requires our willingness to be changed. He is in the business of change – changing the weak to the strong, changing the poor to rich, changing the bowed down to the upright, changing sinners to saints, changing orphans to children of the King. Even if we can't decide to change, we can decide to be changed.

What is the next good decision you can make today? Make sure that decision moves you closer to Jesus.

Song to Consider: "I Have Decided to Follow Jesus"

My Song: When Deeper Gets the Valley

This world brings many trials.
At times, our faith is tested.
Oft' we fail and stumble,
When rugged gets the way.
But keep your eyes on Jesus.
He's waiting there to help you.
Take Him every burden,
And you will hear Him say;

When deeper gets the valley,
Higher gets the mountains.
When deeper gets the valley,
Cooler flows the stream.
The longer you're in a trial,
The sweeter is the victory.
When deeper gets the valley,
The closer gets the Lord.

Now I've had many troubles,
And I've had lots of heartaches.
But I've got my Jesus, and
His glory fills my soul.
So when you're tried and tested,
Just go to him believing.
You'll find him there waiting,
His strength will let you know. (Chorus)

Prayer: Father, You are timeless and see the future now. *I am Yours – I belong to You.* You are great; You are kind; You are good all the time. I am trusting that Your goodness and Your mercies will follow me all the days of my life. Today, I live by faith and decide to follow You one day at a time. I leave the future in Your hands and, by faith, believe that You have a purpose that is best for me. In Jesus' mighty name, Amen.

Give Us this Day

Let's begin by considering these scriptures.

"Give us today our *daily b*read" (Matthew 6:11). [What we need to live]

"So do not worry, saying, 'What shall we eat?' or 'What shall we drink?' or 'What shall we wear?' For the pagans run after all these things, and your heavenly Father knows that you *need t*hem" (Matthew 6:31-32).

"And my God will meet *all your needs* according to the riches of his glory in Christ Jesus" (Philippians 4:19)

"For everything in the world—what our bodies *want*, what our eyes *desire*, and the *pride* of life—comes not from the Father but the world' (1 John 2:16 emphasis added*)*.

There is a real struggle to differentiate between our wants and our needs. In the western world, our culture makes it difficult to prioritize needs and desires. Billions of dollars are spent convincing us that we need what we desire. I have stated before that Jesus will never be all we want, but He will always be all we need. If we are honest, we must admit that God will have no part in some of what we want. While Father has a keen interest in what we need, He will oppose every desire that we prioritize above Him and His purposes.

Let me give you some examples of this struggle. I *want* carrot cake, but I *need e*xercise. I *want* it now, but I *need* patience. I might *want* five million dollars, but I *need* to learn money is a tool, and God is my only security. I may *want* recognition that I feel I deserve, but I may *need t*o learn humility to gain a servant's heart. I may be sick and *want* to be well, but I may *need* to be an instrument of suffering to remind others this is not my final home. I may *want* to be happy with my current situation, but I may *need* to learn joy in every circumstance. I may *want* to be right, but I *need* to give up my rights for the benefit of others. I may *want* more, but I may *need* less so that I can grow a more grateful heart for what I have.

We *need* air to breathe, but we *want* air conditioning. We *need* water to drink, but we *want* a beer. We *need* bread to eat, but we *want* tenderloin. We *need* shelter, but we *want* a mansion. We *want* control of our life, but we *need* God's control to live life abundantly.

Is it possible to get all we want and miss all we need? Jesus said, "If a man gains everything the world has to offer, but loses his eternal soul; what has he profited?" (Matthew 16:26). Unfortunately, the western culture is producing throngs who sink into darkness weighed down by bags of gold, learning all manner of pleasures while dying with an unfillable hole in their heart and hunger in their soul that can't be satisfied.

If we are the instruments of God's good news, we cannot get caught up in what we want. We need Jesus; He is life, joy, peace, love, and self-control. He is the all-powerful instrument of hope and change. In Him, we live, and move, and have our being (significance). He is more precious than silver; more costly than gold; more beautiful than diamonds – and nothing, no nothing, we can ever desire (want) compares to Him.

Consider further:

I may want to give a piece of my mind to someone in an angry tone, but I need *to* use a soft answer in order to be an instrument of God's peace. ***Jesus, provide me all I need to live today.***

I may wan*t* to walk on by that drunken panhandler with a nasty odor, but I need to be an instrument of God's generosity. ***Jesus, provide me all I need to live today.***

I may want to use a beautiful woman to satisfy the lust of my vain imaginations, but I need to be an instrument of God's redemption and wholeness in her life. ***Jesus, provide me all I need to live today.***

I may want discretion, but I need discipline. I may **want** freedom, but I need boundaries. I may want power, but I need to worship. ***Jesus, provide me all I need to live today.***

Song to Consider: "What This World Needs" – Casting Crowns

Prayer: Jesus, be the King of all the kingdoms of my heart today. Teach me to discern the difference between what I want and what I need. Show me Your glory so that I can come to realize that You alone are all that I desire. Give me today all I need to live. Deliver me from the lust of my flesh, the pride of my life, and the schemes of my enemy, the devil. For You and Your Kingdom alone are worthy and all that matters! Amen.

Intentional Christianity

My friend, Ron tells me, "Jesus did not die to make us perfect; He died to make us His." The Christian life is more than a fire insurance policy, more than following a set of rules, more than halos and angels' wings. It is a relationship with the One who loves us more than anyone, anywhere, at any time. I believe the transformed life and God's kingdom is super-natural but it is not magic. Transformation comes through knowing God so intimately the power of His Spirit brings a life filled with righteousness, joy and peace. As I have discussed earlier with you, this is a narrow road. We gain a transformed life when we become _intentional_ in our relationship with Christ.

Too many Christians wait in anguish for a magical transformation, a bolt of lightning or a thunderous voice from the sky to chart their purpose. The Christian life must work in the small things because all of life -- the mountain tops, the valleys and the plains -- are sacred. While God's grace can find us wherever we are, it will never leave us where it found us. Jesus comes into our lives through the front door at our invitation. We become His dwelling place. His righteous presence demands access into every room, every closet, every attic, every basement, until we (His dwelling place) are fit for His dwelling. There is no place for secrets, hidden agendas, backroom deals. How does this transformation happen? Here are four **intentional keys** to experiencing a transformed life.

1. Love God with all our being, love one another and seek God's kingdom first in all of our intentions.

"He answered, '_Love the Lord_ your God with all your heart and with all your soul and with all your strength and with all your mind'; and, '_Love_ your neighbor as yourself'" (Luke 10:27).

"So do not worry, saying, 'What shall we eat?' or 'What shall we drink?' or 'What shall we wear?' For the pagans run after all these things, and your heavenly Father knows that you need them. But seek first his kingdom and his righteousness, and all these things will be given to you as well (Matthew 6:31-33).

2. Intentionally worship the Lord in Spirit and Truth.

"Yet a time is coming and has now come when the true worshipers will worship the Father in the Spirit and in truth, for they are the kind of worshipers the Father seeks. God is spirit, and his worshipers must worship in the Spirit and in truth" (John 4:23-24).

3. Intentionally study God's word to receive understanding how to live a life approved by God.

"I seek you with all my heart; do not let me stray from your commands. I have hidden your word in my heart that I might not sin against you. Praise be to you, LORD; TEACH ME YOUR DECREES" (Psalm 119:10-12).

"Study to show thyself approved unto God, a workman that needs not be ashamed, rightly dividing the word of truth" (II Timothy 2:15).

4. Intentionally take every thought captive under the Lordship of Jesus Christ.

"We demolish arguments and every pretension that set itself up against the knowledge of God, and we take captive every thought to make it obedient to Christ" (2 Corinthians 10:5).

Taking every thought captive takes time, discipline and intention. There is a battle to be fought and won in each of these areas. We must carve out margins of life to regularly engage God in these four intentional keys. For right now, I encourage us to stop waiting for the magic and embrace intentional transformation. The results will be super-natural and exceed our highest expectations. We will fulfill our calling, our purpose, and our destiny. God will meet us in the process and provide the power to succeed in becoming all we are created to be.

What intentional plans have you put in place to know God more intimately?

Song for Consideration: "Oh I Want to Know You More" - Steve Green

My Song: "Song of the Saints"

King of Heaven's Army
Rise up from Your throne,
Lay ruin to every darkness
And win the peace of every troubled heart.

Sovereign prize of glory
Shine brighter than the suns.
Piercing clouds of darkened minds,
That we may see the beauty of Your heart.

The Ruler over every throne
Our Prince of Victory,
Take captive every evil plan
Your courage work in every fearful mind.

Oh precious Lamb of pardon;
The perfect gift from God.
Loose the power of mercy
Bring healing deep in every sin-sick soul.

(Chorus)
Your infinite love
Brings unbounded mercies
To dwell in Your presence -
Unspeakable joy.
The power of Your grace
Transforms broken histories
Making perfect our hearts – making perfect our hearts.

Prayer: Father, Lord Jesus, Holy Spirit, thank You that I belong to You. Thank you for the grace that made me one of Your dearly loved children. Fill me with the desire to know You more and strengthen me to seek after You with all of my being. Give me an insatiable hunger for You, Your Word and Your ways. Make me Your beautiful dwelling place. Make me an instrument of Your purpose. In Jesus' name, Amen.

Forgiven

"Oh, what joy for those whose disobedience is forgiven, whose sin is put out of sight!"

– King David (Psalm 32:1 NLT)

Where Do I Stand?

Prodigal

Remember the story of the prodigal son? This wonderful story of repentance, forgiveness and restoration, found in Luke 15, has been the basis for great teaching and inspiration since Jesus initially shared it with a large group of tax collectors, sinners and Pharisees. I want to share a few thoughts this story has stirred up in my spirit that I believe we can use to live closer to God.

I have wondered why the father never ran after and searched for his son. We see the picture of an aging man waiting anxiously on his porch, hoping against hope that his son would return. Was this all he could do? Didn't the duty of love demand that he search for his son, rescue him from himself and bring him home? How does Father treat us when we demand our own way and run far away?

Since Eden, man has had an urge to demand his own way, manage his own affairs, and then run and hide when he messes it all up. Adam and Eve hid in Eden so that God couldn't see them naked; failing to remember that He had always seen them naked. God called for Adam, "Where are you?" even though He knew exactly where Adam was. He wanted Adam to acknowledge where Adam was to Him.

The vastness of God does not relegate Him to a porch in heaven to anxiously wait for us to return when we stray. His Presence follows us through the sun, rain, darkness, pain, rebellion, frailty and failure. The Psalmist wrote in Psalm 139:

"Where can I go from your Spirit?
  Where can I flee from your presence?
If I go up to the heavens, you are there;
   if I make my bed in the depths, you are there.

If I rise on the wings of the dawn,
  if I settle on the far side of the sea,
even there your hand will guide me,
  your right hand will hold me fast.
If I say, "Surely the darkness will hide me
  and the light become night around me,"
even the darkness will not be dark to you;
  the night will shine like the day,
  for darkness is as light to you."

There have been times in my life that, like the prodigal, I have demanded my way and have run as fast as I could in a direction I thought was away from Father. Sometimes my flight lasted only a few steps; sometimes I ran for years. I have stood in the muck of my mess and contemplated the long journey home asking how do I get back home? Where do I get the strength to return and how far and how long will it take? What I have found, to my great joy, is that, unlike the prodigal father, God's vastness overcomes all time and space. Father is found in the penthouse and the pig sty, in the bar and the prison, in the crack house and the whorehouse, in the lonely alley and the crowded room. You see, when we finally come to our senses and long to return home, regardless of how long or how far we run, the trip back home is quick and short. We only need to turn around, and there is our Father welcoming us with loving arms. Don't fall for the lie that we can run so far we can't get home. When we find ourselves feeling away from God, whether it seems minutes and steps, or years and miles, don't waste time or energy contemplating a hard journey home, simply turn around. HE IS ALWAYS THERE. HE IS EVERYWHERE, and His forgiveness is extravagant.

Scripture:

Luke Chapter 15

Romans 8:38-39: "For I am convinced that neither death nor life, neither angels nor demons, neither the present nor the future, nor any powers, neither height nor depth, nor anything else in all creation, will be able to separate us from the love of God that is in Christ Jesus our Lord."

What are we hiding from God that we know He knows? Why are we hiding it?

Song to Consider: "He Was There All the Time" - Barbara Fairchild

Prayer: Abba, remind me how big You are every day. Help me turn to face You every moment. When I wander, remind me that I am never lost - only facing the wrong direction. Cause me to turn around quickly and relish every moment in Your loving care for in Your Presence is the fullness of joy. Amen.

Guilt and Shame

Have you ever been ashamed of something? Have you ever been ashamed of yourself? I know I have. Shame is a plague on man that has existed since Eden. When Adam and Eve sinned, they suddenly became aware that they had something to hide. They immediately knew that when they faced God, He would see they were different from before. God would see they were guilty. The fact is *they had become guilty.*

Guilty is a legal term. We broke the law; we ran the stop sign; we took someone else's portion, etc. Adam and Eve were suddenly aware they were exposed, and they wanted it covered. They were afraid for God to see them exposed. They became ashamed. Shame is an emotional condition. It is the lie that gets attached to our legal guilt. Shame says you must cover this up. You can still appear innocent even though you are legally guilty. Shame is the imposter of our true selves. Shame is the lie about the facts. The lie says, "You are guilty, and nothing can be done." If we choose to believe the lie, we will live in shame. The shame about shame is that there is no reason for us to live like this. Let me break it down in simple terms.

We are guilty. "For all have sinned and fall short of the glory of God" (Romans 3:23).

We know it. "My guilt has overwhelmed me like a burden too heavy to bear" (Psalm 38:4).

God knows it. "If our hearts condemn us, we know that God is greater than our hearts, and he knows everything (I John 3:20).

Our guilt has been made right by God. "And all are justified freely by his grace through the redemption that came by Christ Jesus" (Romans 3:24).

God can forget our sins even if we can't. "For I will forgive their wickedness and will remember their sins no more" (Hebrews 8:12).

He is not angry with us. "Who is a God like you, who pardons sin and forgives the transgression ….? You do not stay angry forever but delight to show mercy" (Micah 7:18).

There is no need to feel shame over our guilt. For those of us who know Jesus, our verdict is not guilty. Forgiven is our condition. We cannot pay a debt with shame. Jesus took care of our guilt and our shame on the cross. He did not just suffer and die. He was mocked and scorned and hung naked before the gaze of evil men who refused to know mercy. They laughed at His nakedness and gambled for His clothes. The One to who all is exposed bared Himself and endured our shame when He settled our account.

Remember this when you hear the whisper, "You are guilty and you should be ashamed." This voice is not God's. Shout back to the voice, "I know I am guilty, but someone settled my account. I am not ashamed." Then turn to the One who loves you and whisper, "Jesus, You paid it all. All to You I owe. Sin had left a deep dark stain, but You have washed me white as snow."

Scripture: "For it is with your heart that you believe and are justified, and it is with your mouth that you profess your faith and are saved. As Scripture says, 'anyone who believes in him will never be put to shame'" (Romans 10:10-12).

Song to Consider: "What Sin?" - Morgan Cryar

Prayer: Abba, how great is Your love and Your capacity to forgive and forget. Send Your Spirit to help me understand that Your word is true and that I stand chosen, forgiven and loved. Give me the grace to be gentle with myself as I work through all my faults and failures. You have made me new. You have made me better. I am not ashamed of what You are doing in me because of Jesus. Amen

Charges Dismissed

In his book, *The Freedom of Self-Forgetfulness*, Tim Keller states:

> "…Every single day we [our self] are on trial. That is the way everyone's identity works. In the courtroom, you have the prosecution and the defense. And everything we do is providing evidence for the prosecution or evidence for the defense. Some days we feel we are winning the trial and other days we feel we are losing it. But *Paul says that he has found the secret. The trial is over for him. He is out of the courtroom. It is gone. It is over because the ultimate verdict is in.* Now how could that be? Paul puts it very simply. He knows (others) cannot justify him. He knows he cannot justify himself. And what does he say? He says it is the Lord who judges him. It is only his opinion that counts. Do you realize that it is only in the gospel of Jesus Christ that you get the verdict before the performance? In Christianity *the moment we believe him and confess him, God imputes Christ's perfect performance to us as if it was our own, and adopts us into His family*" (Keller 38-39).

I am reminded of a dream I once had. I had somehow slipped into Heaven's courtroom and hid in the back columns where I could see God the Father, the LORD, holding court. My view of the Father was not what Isaiah saw (thus a dream and not a vision), but the LORD was pretty big and impressive with a calm voice, yet so reverberating you could feel it in the marble floors and columns where I was standing. Jesus was up front too. He sat to the right of the LORD before a tremendously big open book.

As I was taking the scene into my puny brain, a sullen, yet impressively dressed being approached the bench or throne. He had the slick look of a Brooklyn lawyer. The LORD spoke, "For what purpose do you approach Me this day? What business do you have here?" The being announced, "Most honorable One, I approach with the recent charges against one known as Ken Dickerson." Now this statement got my attention, and anxiety rose up in me realizing that I was now a party to this proceeding.

The LORD turned to Jesus and said, "My Son, have You any testimony on behalf of this one?" Jesus rose to stand, and looking directly at the back of the room where I was standing, replied, "Yes Father, he is one of Mine and his name is in the book." I sensed great joy and relief, realizing I had found favor with the court. Perhaps this favor would outweigh the charges the sullen one was preparing to bring.

What I dreamed next was a revelation so wonderful that, as I awakened, I was crying quiet tears of joy in the darkness. The LORD turned to the sullen one and said, "You are dismissed from this place with your accusations now as *I will not even hear the charges.*" Suddenly, I was awake.

"For as high as the heavens are above the earth, so great is his love for those who fear him; as far as the east is from the west, so far has *he removed our transgressions from us*" (Psalm 103:11-12 emphasis added).

"This is the covenant I will make with them after that time, says the Lord. I will put my laws in their hearts, and I will write them on their minds." Then he adds: "*Their sins and lawless acts I will remember no more.* And where these have been forgiven, sacrifice for sin is no longer necessary" Hebrews 10:16-18 emphasis added).

Hear me when I say, we must rise to the position of righteousness in our minds and our attitudes so we can effectively offer hope to those around us bent under the accusations of our enemy. We must understand our position as "made righteous." We must continually confess our failures, not for God's accounting, but so we are not seized by shame in our mind and our emotions. The truth is, we are clean; our sins are more than covered – *they are washed away!* Perfect obedience rises from a thankful spirit motivated by great love rather than some worked up sense of duty or the false notion we can earn God's approval. Because we belong to Christ, God has forgotten all our past sins and refuses to hear the case of our present and future sins. OH HAPPY, HAPPY DAY. JESUS WASHED OUR SINS AWAY! CASE DISMISSED!

Song to Consider: "Forgiven And Loved" - Jimmy Needham

Prayer: Thank You, Father, that You have chosen me as one of Your dearly loved children. Break through my mind and into my heart with the truth that I am clean. Jesus paid it all in full. You remember my sins no more and refuse to hear the case brought against me by my accuser. Let me serve and obey You from a pure and thankful heart motivated by love. You bore my guilt; You bore my shame. Raise me up in righteousness to the praise of Your glory and fill me with the power of grace to do what I have been called to do. In Jesus' name, Amen.

Desperate

"Two men went up to the house of God to pray. One of them was a proud religious law-keeper. The other was a man who gathered taxes. The proud religious law-keeper stood and prayed to himself like this, '_God, I thank You that I am not like other men._ I am not like those who steal. I am not like those who do things that are wrong. I am not like those who do sex sins. _I am not even like this tax-gatherer._ I go without food two times a week so I can pray better. I give one-tenth part of the money I earn.' But the man who gathered taxes stood a long way off. He would not even lift his eyes to heaven. But he hit himself on his chest and said, 'God, have mercy on me! I am a sinner!' I tell you, this man went back to his house forgiven, and not the other man" (Luke 18:10-14 emphasis added).

If we are to stay desperate in our need for God's grace and mercy and His intervention in our daily affairs, it is important that we measure ourselves and others in a consistent manner. It is important that we measure ourselves and others by God's standards. A key to humility is an honest view of how we measure up. We (humans) have a tendency to measure and judge sin using a ruler when, truthfully, God measures sin more like the bar on a pole vault. His assessment of the condition of our flesh, as it relates to Jesus' righteousness, is "you are" or "you are not"; not "you came real close", or "you missed by a long shot." As far as mankind is concerned, there is no one righteous, no – not even one.

We have a tendency to use a different ruler when we measure our sin versus the sins of others. We measure our white lies and covetous thoughts with the weight of a feather while we measure murder and adultery with the weight of a ship's anchor. The truth is that our white lies and covetous thoughts weigh a ton in comparison to the bar of Jesus' sinless perfection. You see, if we gain God's view from eternity, we realize that the distance between the best and the worst of us (humans) can fit on the tip of a pin when compared to how far Jesus had to bend down to reach us in our sin and carry our offenses. Paul told the Romans "…all have sinned and fallen short of the glory of God," (Romans 3:23) and went on further to declare, "…the wages of sin is death"(Romans 6:23). Rest assured that a white lie will drag us to hell just as sure as if we murdered our brother.

Desperation will never allow us to elevate ourselves to the position of judge. Our poor judgment happens when we use the wrong ruler or scale to measure sin. Desperation leaves us to plead constantly for mercy. Desperation leaves us to extend consistent mercy. Desperate saints/sinners understand that "where sin abounds, grace does much more abound" (Romans 5:20). Desperate saints/sinners can equally extend that grace to themselves and others. Desperate saints/sinners lay down our rocks and embrace a sinner while encouraging them with, "Let me show you how I found a better way to live." Desperate saints/sinners want mercy so badly that we are quick to extend mercy knowing that "the merciful are blessed by obtaining mercy" (Matthew 5:7).

Desperate saints/sinners understand, "*BE STILL and know My name is mercy. I have chosen you. Know how far I came to find you, all I paid to redeem you, the grace it takes to keep you, the power of My affection, and the focus of My perfect desire.*"

Desperate saints/sinners live in the all-consuming gaze of the eyes of compassion and rest in the mighty arms of amazing grace. Desperate saints/sinners spend so much time inviting others to come in from the cold and enjoy the warmth of our Father's heart that we have little time to judge the measure of another's guilt.

We press on down the path knowing Romans 5:6-11:

> "When we were utterly helpless, Christ came at just the right time and died for us, sinners. Now, most people would not be willing to die for an upright person, though someone might perhaps be willing to die for a person who is especially good. But God showed his great love for us by sending Christ to die for us while we were still sinners. And since we have been made right in God's sight by the blood of Christ, he will certainly save us from God's condemnation. For since our friendship with God was restored by the death of his Son while we were still his enemies, we will certainly be saved through the life of his

Son. So now we can rejoice in our wonderful new relationship with God because our Lord Jesus Christ has made us friends of God"(New Living Translation).

And we will be friends of sinners because our Lord Jesus Christ is the friend of sinners.

Song to Consider: "Jesus Friend of Sinners" – Casting Crowns

Prayer: Gracious Father, give me the grace to roll up my scroll of accusations and lay down my stones of punishment. Remind me daily of the grace and mercy I have received and how far You came to find and save me. Help me love like You love and always remember it is Your kindness that leads to repentance. I know Your name is Mercy and that the same grace that found me is always searching for others who need a touch from You. In Jesus' name, Amen.

Stay desperate friends -- desperate for mercy, desperate for God!

What Does It Cost?

The Power of the Cross

I was driving to an appointment today when the small wooden cross hanging from the chain of my rearview mirror caught my attention. This cross was made by my wife Jeanenne's Uncle, Dwight, and has been hanging in my truck for years. It's funny how things in such proximity to us become so familiar we fail to give them a second thought. We have crosses on our walls and crosses on our mantles, crosses hanging from suction cups on our windows and crosses on our television. We are surrounded by crosses so familiar they are missed in our consciousness. This morning the cross caught my eye, then my attention, then my spirit, as it danced ever so slightly to the rhythm of the freeway.

The simple cross in my truck is a lovely piece of handiwork. Today its beauty took me by surprise. I thought of the cross that Jesus hung on and surmised that it was not beautiful at all. Perhaps it had been a tool of punishment and execution on many occasions before this Good Friday. Could the King of Glory die on a used cross?

Contrary to many popular descriptions, Jesus probably carried only the crossbeam to Golgotha. There He was nailed through the hands, lashed to the crossbeam by ropes and then hoisted up into an elevated position before they nailed His feet. Roman crosses were not beautiful; they struck fear in the mind as a reminder for all subject to the empire's laws that the state would brutally deal with crimes. The amazing thing is that this one execution turned the Roman's ugly symbol of violent punishment and death into a symbol of peace, hope and life for millions of people through the next two millennia, and likely hundreds of millions of Jesus' followers alive today. This reality pierced my mind and heart. I paused to give thanks, through moist eyes, while making sure I stayed in my lane. More than that, I considered what this lovely little cross meant to me.

First, I remembered who I belong to and the price that was paid to purchase me. God poured out on earth the most precious treasure of heaven, the best of His love, the only righteous one to pay the price that justice required for my adoption to His family. He took in His body my sin and my sickness and spilled out His innocent blood required to seal God's best covenant. He did this for as many as would receive Him or as few as would receive Him - *even if I was the only one.* Transgression demanded that innocence balance the scale. I could not pay, but Jesus settled the debt.

Second, I need to begin each day remembering the cross. I need to cherish it, to honor it, to give it more than just a passing glance. It represents a sea change in the destiny of mankind. It represents a sea change in my destiny. It represents the Good News that God is not angry; He is full of grace, mercy and love, and He proved it at the cross. In all of this, the cross has indeed become a beautiful and lovely thing.

Finally, I remembered that this cross was empty. Not a crucifix, just an empty cross (I have no quarrel with a crucifix). My heart leaps with joy to remember - not in my mind but my inner being - He is not there anymore. The Christ we serve is not hanging from an ugly tree; the Christ we serve has come down from the cross and come up from the grave and rules all creation with power and authority at the right hand of Jehovah. The Apostle John saw his lifeless body on Calvary and later he saw Him again as King of kings and Lord of lords on Patmos as recorded in the Revelation. At His feet we worship; at His feet, all will bow.

Do you have a cross? Where do you keep it? When is the last time its presence pierced your mind? I am thankful to be surrounded by many crosses. I will not let their beauty go long without my notice again.

Scripture: "Therefore, since we are surrounded by such a great cloud of witnesses, let us throw off everything that hinders and the sin that so easily entangles. And let us run with perseverance the race marked out for us, fixing our eyes on Jesus, the Pioneer, and Perfecter of our faith. For the joy set before him, he endured the cross, scorning its shame, and sat down at the right hand of the throne of God. Consider him who endured such opposition from sinners, so that you will not grow weary and lose heart" (Hebrews 12:1-3)."He himself bore our sins" in his body on the **cross**, so that we might die to sins and live for righteousness; "by his wounds you have been healed" (I Peter 2:24).

Song to Consider: "The Power of the Cross" - Keith and Kristyn Getty

My Song: Come and See

There is a fountain; Oh come and see,
Flowing from the heart of Jesus
Down a hill called Calvary.
And those who plunge in,
Can be set free.
Finding pardon for a sinner,
And a home for every stranger,
Filled with light and life and joy abundantly.

Oh, come and see.

There is a kingdom, Oh come and see,
It was built by God the Father,
It will last eternally.
And when you enter,
Come see the King.
Jesus is a friend of sinners,
He sticks closer than a brother
Filled with light and life and shelter in his wings.
Oh, come and see.

Prayer: Lord Jesus, burn into my spirit the image of the cross. Remind me often of what took place there and the difference it has made for me. Let me rejoice that it is empty now and You are powerfully exalted. Let me embrace it as a beautiful instrument of life, joy and peace. For Your sake, Amen.

Mercy is a Messy Enterprise

I was privileged to worship across the bridge at Faith Farm in Boynton Beach one Sunday. Pastor Jim shared about going to God's throne of grace to obtain mercy. In the days since, I have often thought about the business of mercy. How is it obtained, how is it shared, how is it traded, and how is it given? Before I share my recent thoughts, let's look at some important messages on mercy in the Scriptures.

> "When Moses had proclaimed every command of the law to all the people, he took the blood of calves, together with water, scarlet wool and branches of hyssop, and *sprinkled the scroll and all the people.* He said, 'This is the blood of the covenant, which God has commanded you to keep.' In the same way, *he sprinkled with the blood both the tabernacle and everything used in its ceremonies.* In fact, the law requires that nearly everything be cleansed with blood and *without the shedding of blood there is no forgiveness*" (Hebrews 9:19-22 emphasis added).

> "Speak and act as those who are going to be judged by the law that gives freedom, because *judgment without mercy will be shown to anyone who has not been merciful. Mercy triumphs over judgment*" (James 2:12-13 emphasis added).

> "Blessed are the merciful, for they will be shown mercy" (Matthew 5:7).

> *"But the tax collector stood at a distance. He would not even look up to heaven, but beat his breast and said, 'God, have mercy on me, a sinner.'* I tell you that *this man*, rather than the other, *went home justified before God"* (Luke 18:13-14 emphasis added).

When I think of what consistently took place in the Old Testament year after year, generation after generation, where the Hebrews killed and sacrificed millions of animals to cover their sins, I must confess some repulsion to this awful business. Can you imagine the smells and sights of this process – all the slaughter and draining, field dressing and burning? It had to bear the resemblance of a battlefield. Jehovah ordained this ritual practice to picture the hideous, revolting, stinking mess of the iniquity of humanity. All of this sacrifice resulted in mercy for the nation of Israel. They would avoid getting what they really deserved; their sins were covered again and again. *Mercy is a messy enterprise.*

Resolving and paying for all that is wrong is not easy, nor is it pretty. Jesus, the perfect Lamb of God, was abused, mutilated and tortured to death in public view where He hung naked and humiliated before His friends and His foes. Perfection was battered and bloodied to provide a solution to God's demand of how to handle sin. The perfect answer to reconcile love and justice was broken and spilled out to resolve the question of mercy. Our pain traded for peace, and judgment traded for grace on an instrument of punishment. Jesus received the judgment we deserved so that we could gain a Father and a home to which we had no claim. *Mercy is a messy enterprise.*

We dare not think that we can escape the messy business of mercy. Having obtained mercy, we must stand ready to practice it and all that it demands. God's mercy must be passed on to those who don't think like us, look like us, act like us, smell like us, or talk like us. Mercy is not a comfortable demand. It requires a walk through the stench of unpleasant circumstances to be ministers of grace, peace, truth, and reconciliation in places we may not want to go. It requires us to hold our tongues, stretch out our arms and suffer the pain of rejection at the hands of people we don't even like. It requires us to hate the sin while loving those that practice it, remembering the mercy shown to us. *Mercy is a messy enterprise.*

Sow the seeds of mercy if you need mercy. As we move forward to meet the demands of mercy, let's remember that the merciful will receive mercy in the same measure they give it. Let's remember what James shared in chapter two of his book, *"Mercy triumphs over judgment"* (James 2:13).

Song to Consider: "Seek Justice, Love Mercy" – Me In Motion Doug McKelvey/Seth Mosley

Prayer: Father, help me always to remember what it cost You and Your Son to pay for the mess of my sin. Help me to be willing to look beyond the mess of others' faults and minister mercy and grace. Give me Your heart to move me in the ministry of mercy as I learn each day that mercy triumphs over judgment and perfect love covers a multitude of sins. For Jesus' sake, Amen

Wounds that Never Heal

I have been thinking about the appearance of Jesus to His disciples the evening after His resurrection. Jesus suddenly appears among them in His supernatural resurrected body. A body able to appear and disappear, yet He still bore the open wounds from His crucifixion in His hands and side and feet.

> "While they were still talking about this, Jesus himself stood among them and said to them, 'Peace be with you.' They were startled and frightened, thinking they saw a ghost. He said to them, 'Why are you troubled, and why do doubts rise in your minds? _Look at my hands and my feet._ It is I myself! Touch me and see; a ghost does not have flesh and bones, as you see I have.' When he had said this, he showed them his hands and feet" (Luke 24:38-40).

In a later appearance, Jesus admonishes Thomas to put his hand in His side wound. Jesus had a transformed, resurrected body that still had the wounds of His passion (suffering) in it.

> "Then he said to Thomas, 'Put your finger here; see my hands. _Reach out your hand and put it into my side._ Stop doubting and believe'" (John 20:27 emphasis added).

The Apostle John's Revelation vision on Patmos tells us that Jesus, enthroned and worshiped in heaven, still bears these wounds.

> "Then I saw a Lamb, _looking as if it had been slain,_ standing at the center of the throne, encircled by the four living creatures and the elders…"(Revelation 5:6).

I wonder why these wounds of His crucifixion never heal. What does this mean for us who come to Christ broken, wounded, sinful and weak (which is the only way we can approach Christ – out of desperate need)? Consider Isaiah's prophetic words:

> "Surely he took up our pain and bore our suffering, yet we considered him punished by God, stricken by him, and

afflicted. But he was pierced for our transgressions; he was crushed for our iniquities; the punishment that brought us peace was on him, and *by his wounds we are healed*" (Isaiah 53:4-6 emphasis added).

Isaiah is saying that, while *we* considered Jesus being stricken and punished by God, He was *punished by us* and bore our pain, suffering and transgressions. *His wounds brought us peace and healing.*

These wounds of Jesus have never healed; they are still borne in His transformed resurrected body to offer us peace and healing. These wounds are the ornaments of His obedience, His sacrifice, His ability to satisfy divine justice and redeem fallen men. They remain the source from which grace and mercy flow to us from God the Father's heart through Jesus' wounds and on to desperate sinners needing redemption and healing. In all His regal splendor, Christ sits at the right hand of God in heaven. Without a word, He raises His wounded hands, to the wonderment of angels and the worship of saints, as a sign that sings like the old spiritual hymn, "There is a balm in Gilead, to make the wounded whole. There is a balm in Gilead, to heal the sin-sick soul."

What does this mean for us? What about our wounds? What about the wounds we bear that never heal? We are all wounded in some way -- physically, emotionally and even spiritually. Some are superficial scrapes and scratches that are easily forgotten and easily relieved. Some are deep and painful, continuing to ooze hurt and unpleasantness. I have lived long enough with some of my wounds that I honestly feel they will never heal this side of Heaven.

What do Jesus' open wounds provide for me? First, they remind me that I am still subject to pain. Even though I am redeemed, and a child of God, living in this world can be painful and still inflict deep wounds. What will my response be when I am wounded? As I look to my LORD in Heaven, He reaches out with wounded hands to remind me there is grace and there is mercy for the wounded and the wounder. I can pass on grace and mercy to those who wound me just as it is passed to me and through me by my Wounded Champion.

Next, these unhealed wounds of Jesus bring me hope. Hope that there is relief from the sadness and disappointment both in this life and in the life to come. Hope that the never-ending eternal power of the blood of Christ brings to bear on my failures and disappointments. Whether it is disappointment or failure, the past is dealt with, today is dealt with, and the future is dealt with by love, forgiveness, atonement, grace, and mercy that never, ever run out. *What Jesus endured two thousand years ago is still active today for my benefit – and yours too.*

Finally, what am I to make of my wounds that will never heal? Paul told the Romans, "I consider that our present sufferings are not worth comparing with the glory that will be revealed in us" (Romans 8:18). With these words, I can reconcile my pain, and I can forgive those that bring me pain. Not only can I forgive them, but I can make peace with them. Isaiah says, "The punishment Christ endured brought us peace." So Jesus' wounds that never heal can heal our wounds and, for those that are not, can allow us to come to peace with the "wounders" that inflict them. That's great news if we come to the understanding that there is not a life that can avoid all pain. However, there is a life that can live in peace with a grateful heart that channels grace and mercy flowing from Father's heart through the wounds of Jesus that never heal. There is a life that considers its scars, not as remembrances of failure and pain, but as marks of ownership by One who endured what we could never endure so that we, in turn, can endure with joy, forever in His presence.

Song to Consider: "The Hurt and the Healer" – Mercy Me

Prayer: Lord Jesus, a river of life flows from Your heart that brings healing, forgiveness, joy, and peace. Thanks for the eternalness of Your wounds that bring peace and healing. May the wounds I bear be vessels to receive from the wounds You bear the power of grace and mercy. The grace and mercy for me and for those I have the opportunity to live with every day. As I live my life in this world, help me quickly bring my afflictions and my failures to Your wounded hands for healing. May I reckon the scars from this life as signs of Your ownership and Your work within me for Your glory and the sake of Your Kingdom's cause, Amen.

The Road Less Traveled

We kid ourselves if we think the Kingdom life on earth is always an easy, carefree journey. This thinking sets us up for great disappointment when trouble comes our way. The gift of everlasting life and abundant life is free, but following Jesus is hard. Beside this, we live in a broken world. One day God will restore the order of Eden to the earth, but right now He is in the business of fixing people. The world gets fixed only to the extent that we get fixed, and we can affect our world around us. In this world, heartache, hopelessness, and downright meanness fill up the majority of people's lives every day. In Christ we have peace, but we will experience tribulation in our lives. We will endure trials to strengthen our patience and our faith. Many will despitefully use us for no other reason than we have become peculiar people. We will experience sickness, and ultimately our bodies are going to grow old, wear out and die. However, if we develop our spiritual eyes and our spiritual ears, and faithfully listen to God's voice - He will encourage, comfort and always come to our aide. We will receive unspeakable joy even when we may lack happiness.

Sadly, the road to hell and disappointment is one broad freeway that, the majority of humans travel. So much of humanity speeds recklessly along this broad road leaving devastation in their wake. The road leading away from God is most often the path of least resistance. The road to Heaven is the road less traveled. It is the path with thorns and stones, valleys and steep grades. It is the path that we choose to travel when we leave the freeway to nowhere and decide to follow Jesus. However, if we look closely, we can recognize the path, much of the overgrowth has been pulled aside by the weight of a dragging cross. We can find our way because God's Son dragged His cross along this path and then many who, like us, deciding to follow Him, pulled their crosses along the way. When we see the path rutted with the marks of heavy crosses, we can walk in the confidence that many had gone this way before and finished the journey. At times, when the path gets a little wider, we can see a glimpse of the end of the journey. Abba waits and calls with an encouraging voice, "Come to Me. I know you are going to make it," and we hear Christ say, "Keep walking. I will pick you up when you stumble and even carry you when you faint." The path is narrow, often rough and steep, and the journey, by design, carefully considered. But it is the right way, the way that leads somewhere - the way that leads us toward home.

> I shall be telling this with a sigh
> Somewhere ages and ages hence:
> Two roads diverged in a wood, and I,
> I took the one less traveled by,
> And that has made all the difference.

– Robert Frost

THE PATHWAY OF JESUS MAKES ALL THE DIFFERENCE!!

Scriptures

"You can enter God's Kingdom only through the narrow gate. The highway to hell is broad, and its gate is wide for the many who choose that way. But the gateway to life is very narrow and the road is difficult, and only a few ever find it" (Matthew 7:13-14 NLT).

"If any of you wants to be my follower, you must give up your own way, take up your cross, and follow me. If you try to hang on to your life, you will lose it. But if you give up your life for my sake, your will save it" (Matthew 16: 24-25 NLT). "I have told you these things so that in me you may have peace. In this world, you will have trouble. But take heart! I have overcome the world" (John 16:33).

"Consider it pure joy, my brothers and sisters, whenever you face trials of many kinds because you know that the testing of your faith produces perseverance. Let perseverance finish its work so that you may be mature and complete, not lacking anything" (James 1:2-4).

Song to Consider: "Blessings" by Laura Story

Prayer: Abba, Your love, mercy, grace, and sovereign hand sustain us through the best and worst of life. Keep us on the road less traveled and help us understand that the way of least resistance often leads to nowhere. You hear us when we call; You help us when we fall; You even carry us when we are too weary to face another mile on the rough road. Help us rejoice that You cut the trail, and many others have completed the course before us. Thank You - that amidst all the stubble, thorns, tight spots, and steep grades, we can be sure this path leads home to where You are, Amen.

May the love of Christ seize all of you with His powerful affection.

How Does It Work?

The Essence of Repentance

I have been thinking a lot about how true repentance looks. C. S. Lewis had much to say about repentance. In many cases, it was his opinion that, we ask God to excuse our sins rather than forgive our sins. We go to Him with the attitude that says, "You know the way I am. Can You cover me this time?" rather than with an attitude of Godly sorrow and a determination that, with His help, we are going to change our way of thinking and acting. Paul told the church in Corinth that, sorrow brings repentance that leads to salvation and leaves no regret, but worldly sorrow brings death" (2 Cor. 7:10). True repentance is the key to radical change that brings abundant and everlasting life. It is the difference between suicide and significance. The Apostle Paul told King Agrippa that, "he preached to those in Damascus, Jerusalem, Judea and all the Gentiles that they should repent and turn to God and then demonstrate their repentance by their deeds" (Acts 26:20).

I love the story of Zacchaeus. He was the gangster of Jericho. Everyone despised him with good reason. In the name of Rome, he would threaten, extort and always get extra on the side. Robbing, cheating and lying were the attributes of his profession, and on top of all of this, he was a "wee little man." Check this out.

> "Jesus entered Jericho and was passing through. A man was there by the name of Zacchaeus; he was a chief tax collector and was wealthy. He wanted to see who Jesus was, but because he was short, he could not see over the crowd. So he ran ahead and climbed a sycamore-fig tree to see him since Jesus was coming that way. When Jesus reached the spot, he looked up and said to him, "Zacchaeus, come down immediately. I must stay at your house today." So he came down at once and welcomed him gladly. All the people saw this and began to mutter, "He

has gone to be the guest of a sinner." But Zacchaeus stood up and said to the Lord, "Look, Lord! Here and now I give half of my possessions to the poor, and if I have cheated anybody out of anything, I will pay back four times the amount." Jesus said to him, "Today salvation has come to this house, because this man, too, is a son of Abraham. For the Son of Man came to seek and to save the lost" (Luke 19:1-10).

Over twenty-five years ago, God woke me in the night under great conviction saying, "You are a thief and it's time to deal with it." I wrestled for days with this accusation until I could not take the sorrow any longer. I cried to God, "What is it You want me to do?" He said, "Confess, repent and make it right." You see, I had stolen money from my former employer and had never gotten caught. But this had grieved God and left me with a guilty conscience that clouded my life. It was time to get free. I confessed this to my pastor, but God demanded that I had to stand up and confess it to the entire church and promise to make amends by repaying all I had stolen. I contacted my former employer and arranged to account for and repay the stolen money. Restoration came at a great monetary cost to my family. They would go without some things because of it. I remember the President of my former employer telling me, "God must be preparing you for His purposes; this is the evidence of true repentance." I have never forgotten his words.

Three things happened to Zacchaeus when he encountered Jesus. First, he realized he had touched true righteousness that demanded a radical change in him. He realized that this righteousness had sought him out of a crowd and confronted him in a personal way, and that this relationship required a change in thinking and a change in behavior. Secondly, Zacchaeus realized that this righteousness he had touched demanded a confession of the things that made him unrighteous and a public recanting of his public and private sins. Finally, he realized that the only way that others could believe he had changed was to show the fruit of repentance by making amends. He would repay all he had wronged with interest. Furthermore, he recanted his self-centered greed and testified of a new and generous heart by giving to the poor. Jesus pronounced that salvation had come to his house. The one who was wretched and despised by all of Jericho became an acknowledged friend of God.

To the child of God, repentance becomes a way of life. Our relationship to righteousness is unrelenting in its demands for constant and complete repentance. We grieve when we sin against God and others whether or not we get caught, knowing that God can't use an unrepentant life to change an unrepentant world. We then set our will to fix the things we break and restore the things we take when we fall short of the righteousness that has come to seek us out and visit with us on a constant basis.

Rosaria Champagne Butterfield, the author of *The Secret Thoughts of an Unlikely Convert* shares, "There is only one thing to do when you meet the Living God; you must fall on your face and repent of your sins. Repentance is a bittersweet business. Repentance is not just a conversion exercise -- it is the posture of the Christian, much like 'tree' or 'full lotus' is the posture of the Yogi. Repentance is our daily fruit, our hourly washing, our minute by the minute wake-up call, our reminder of God's creation, Jesus' blood, and the Holy Spirit's comfort. Repentance is the only no-shame solution to a renewed Christian conscience because it only proves obvious: God was right all along."

Song to Consider: "I Repent" – Steve Green

Prayer: Father, Jesus, Holy Spirit, thank You that You have sought me out and chosen to visit me with Your righteousness. Make repentance the posture of my life that I can draw close to Your perfect heart every day. Give me strength to see, acknowledge and confess my faults with a determination to, with Your help, restore all I may break and all I that I may take along the way. Keep me from offering excuses for the way I am and to quickly return to fall in love with You when I briefly stray or step away. Help me always give reconciliation and forgiveness a chance by making peace rather than strife and sowing the fruit of repentance whenever I cause pain to others. I confess that *You alone* can make a perfect heart; please do this within me today and every day. For Your Kingdom's cause, Amen.

The Ministry of Reconciliation

Some time ago, I was fortunate to hear Archbishop Desmond Tutu speak at the national *Leadercast*. In remembering Nelson Mandela, the Archbishop brought to mind a fact that few of us remembered because of Mandela's much heralded heroic role in the dismantling of apartheid after his release from a twenty-seven year prison term in 1990. Tutu reminded us that when first imprisoned, Mandela was a very angry man who advocated even the use of violence in the fight against racial injustice. In his argument against the notion that Mandela's years in prison became lost opportunity, the Archbishop shared how Mandela was transformed into a peacemaker during this time and emerged fully equipped to lead the quest to transform South Africa's discrimination legacy. Mandela insisted on reconciliation through confession and forgiveness because he realized that this process was the only way both parties, the wounded and the "wounders," would ever be able to look each other in the eye and live in peace. The Archbishop stood alongside Mandela in this process. There was a radical change in Mandela from a peace-demander to a peacemaker. A perceived troublemaker changed into a transformational leader.

This testimony has produced much thought in me. We are called to be peacemakers and ministers of reconciliation. If we are to be successful, it will take a deep understanding of the principle that, if Jesus' blood is sufficient to wash away the sins of the world, His blood will not only wash away the sins we have committed, but it will wash away the sins committed against us. We have to engage in both parts of this provision to be peacemakers and bring reconciliation. Our brokenness leaves sharp edges that cut those we are near when we live careless, self-centered or rebellious lives. How do we make peace? How do we reconcile with our family, our friends and our foes? How do we get to where we can look everyone in the eye and honestly say, God loves you, I love you, be ye reconciled to God? How can we minister reconciliation if we cannot achieve reconciliation inside of us?

Reconciliation has two parts: giving forgiveness and asking forgiveness. We are called to become proficient in both parts.

"But when you are praying, first **forgive** anyone you are holding a grudge against, so that your Father in heaven will **forgive** your sins, too" (Mark 11:25).

"So if you are presenting a sacrifice at the altar in the Temple and *you suddenly remember that someone has something against you,* leave your sacrifice there at the altar. *Go and be reconciled (apologize) to that person.* Then come and offer your sacrifice to God" (Matthew 5: 23-24 emphasis added).

If there is tension between parties, peace will come when forgiveness is asked for and given. An apology is required. It is the hard work of making peace. You see, as hard as forgiveness is, we are acknowledging another's faults. Reconciliation requires we go beyond forgiveness and acknowledge our faults. It is the courage to make peace by tearing down the walls we have erected and beginning to remove the supports that prohibit others from tearing down their walls. Making amends is a two-edged peacemaking sword. I must not only forgive, but I must ask for forgiveness. Making amends is hard. This is transparency, and this is vulnerability. We master confession and apologize to God when we realize He is forgiving, but apologies to others may not be so easily received. However, an apology opens the door for forgiveness by the offended. It is the opening salvo in the quest for lasting peace. Remember we are to be peacemakers, not peacekeepers. We can keep the peace by staying away from relationships. We are commanded to make peace by the Prince of Peace. We are commanded to live in relationship with family, friend, and foe. We are called to "go into the world" so that Christ's kingdom comes here on earth, in everything we touch every day.

Real apologies contain specific terms. An apology that brings healing must be specific. If we know we have offended someone, the "I'm sorry if I have offended you" will not bring peace. We must remove the "if" from the equation and identify the offense. A much better stated apology is, "Please forgive me for (identify the offense)" or if we suspect we have offended, "Please tell me how I have offended you." Verbalizing the offense brings the power of confession to the process.

Nelson Mandela emerged from prison with a commitment to peace and reconciliation. He took on a new role as "healer of the wounds" in his nation. Many people spend even longer than twenty-seven years in prison to their anger and wounded hearts. The truth is that evil resides in unforgiveness. It causes us, while living near others, to question motives, feed pettiness and accentuate our differences rather than dwelling in unity. We cannot change the world around us while we live in discord and suspicion. Real peace comes with giving and asking forgiveness and a willingness to practice as often as required. I know in my case, they are required almost every day. Lately, I have been required to apologize to many people, some of them I offended decades ago. I want you to hold me accountable when I offend you. I will apologize when confronted with my offenses because I want to spend the rest of my life as an instrument of peace and reconciliation. Let's walk together in the power that comes from really believing that Jesus paid for all sins – those we commit and those committed against us.

To whom do you need to apologize? Will you make yourself vulnerable to make reconciliation possible? Make a list of offenses you have carried out and make a list of offenses committed against you. Confess to God that you will act on the faith that Jesus' blood has covered both lists.

Song to Consider: "Song of Reconciliation" – Wayne Kirkpatrick

Prayer: Father, give me the courage to launch the quest for peace with the words "I am sorry." Give me the strength to tear down walls of separation; give me the power to overcome injury with a pardon. Strengthen me to make peace by engaging the brokenness around me and, most importantly, by engaging the brokenness I have created. For the sake of the One You have sent to cover our sins and bind our broken hearts, Jesus the Prince of Peace, Amen.

Contract or Covenant

We live in a complicated culture and society today. Individuals and businesses spend large sums of money with lawyers who write contracts that bind two or more parties together and assure fairness and behavior that fulfills the contract. Even with all of this care and expense, we learn daily about broken contracts -- failure to perform, failure to pay, failure to be timely. Contracts have become necessary to our way of life. The problem with contracts is that if one party fails to live up to their obligation, the contract is broken. Many contracts provide that the failure of one party to fulfill their part releases the other party or parties from obligation for their part. Much of our culture is transactional; we expect fairness, value and honesty. Many times these are not realized because of the inability of the other party to live up to their end of the bargain. Sincerity does not always translate into success. We live in a broken world.

The Kingdom of God is built, not on the principles of contracts, but on the principles of covenants. Knowing the state of fallen man, God realized that a contract would never keep man and God together. Man, in his fallen state, would always fall short of the terms of the contract out of unwillingness or inability to meet the terms. God handed down the Law to Moses - a contract man could not keep. The nation of Israel failed over and over to fulfill the obligations of the law. If God was going to restore the fellowship enjoyed in Eden, He would have to establish a relationship based on His willingness and His abilities alone to keep the relationship intact. He sent Christ to, once and for all, cover our inabilities and unwillingness to fulfill our contract with God. Through Christ, the Father established a covenant that would not fail because its terms were simply, _"I will love and hold on to you - even if you can't or won't hold on to Me."_ With an established covenant, the failure on the part of one party can no longer break the relationship. Both parties must fail to break a covenant - and God cannot fail.

Our role as peacemakers, grace-givers and mercy-workers requires us to think in covenant rather than contractual terms. We must show the power of the cross and the unconditional love of God in our relationships by establishing and maintaining covenants that state: "I will love and hold on to you - even if you can't or won't hold on to me." Our culture and society fail on so many accounts today because it treats covenant relationships like contracts. Marriages and families disintegrate with attitudes that disregard the covenant principle. To walk in covenant principles is hard but the outcome is precious.

In covenant, we experience the giving and receiving of the heart of Abba. It requires the manifest gifts of God's Spirit: love, joy, peace, kindness, self-control, truth-telling, and forgiveness. These are the things we have been given by our Father through Christ because of His covenant heart. We will know the perfect joy of Abba when we learn to hold on to each other -- even when the other can't or won't hold on to us.

In my lifetime, I have been both a covenant breaker and a covenant keeper. I have lived to see the fruit of both ways of life. Broken covenants reap a large and bitter harvest. Kept covenants reap unspeakable joy. *Let's commit to covenant relationships in all of life.* Let's commit that we will hold on to each other in the good times and the bad times as we remember the unfailing hand always holding on to us.

Scripture:

"The Holy Spirit also testifies to us about this. First, he says: 'This is the covenant **I** will make with them after that time, says the Lord. *I will put my laws in their hearts, and I will write them on their minds.'* Then he adds: 'Their sins and lawless acts I will remember no more.' And where these have been forgiven, sacrifice for sin is no longer necessary" (Hebrews 10:15-18 emphasis added).

Word for Contemplation: Covenant -- a solemn agreement between members to act together in harmony within their relationship

What are the results of your broken covenants? How many people were affected?

What are the results of your kept covenants? How many people are affected?

God has graciously made provision for our inabilities to keep covenant. He is a miraculous healer, and He can make all things new.

Song to Consider: "Hold You Up" - Matthew West

Prayer: Abba, You hold on to us even when we can't or won't hold on to You. You understand our frailties and make allowance for our weakness. Give us the strength to keep our vows and be people of our word. Fill us with Your love and the commitment to hold on to those we are in a relationship with even when they might lose their grip. Greater love has no man than to lay down his life for his friends. Help us to love greatly and bring us the unspoiled fruit of being promise keepers. In Jesus' Name, Amen.

The Rest of the (Easter) Story

As I write, I am basking in the glory of Spring. The long, hard, cold winter has given way to warmth and life appearing in the beautiful hues of yellow, green and light blue. Even the cold temperatures of the past two days can't dim the fact that renewal is coming out everywhere. I can smell the fresh cut grass and see the small buds growing on the bushes. The spring definitely increases my energy and lightens my mood. Several birthdays are arriving in short order, and they remind me of how special my family is. We are fortunate to have each other, our health, our safety, our jobs, and our faith. My mind is drawn to Resurrection week and the events we remember during the week. It is a week that changed the history of the world. One man's death and resurrection from the dead turned the known world on its calendar. God had drawn near to mankind; mankind had killed God's Son and God opened Heaven to all those who would believe by raising His Son from the dead. Let me share what I am thinking about this week. Please don't quibble about theology as this is just the heart imaginings of a romantic sinner basking in the light of amazing grace. These are little snippets in my heart that I would not normally think.

Can you imagine the agony of Mary when John led her away from Golgotha, the lifeless, butchered body of her son hanging on the executioner's instrument of death? The whisper of the angel, "This is God's boy; Call Him Jesus; He will save" etched in her mind; the memories of an angel choir and the birthday gifts brought by kings who bowed down before her baby's bed, all shattered by the stark events of this darkened afternoon. A promised King betrayed by hypocrites and slaughtered by men that scoffed at mercy and practiced cruelty with precision. She had seen her son die. Had God died with Him? Had God died in Him? Despair raged against the promise of Messiah. Her grief swallowed up the miracles of the water and the wine, the healing of the lame, the joy of seeing Lazarus alive. These seemed so long ago. Who would save Israel now? Who would save her family now? Who would save her now? In the darkness doubt called to her heart, "Was this all to no avail?"

An unexplained earthquake had stirred up dusty air that delayed the returning sunlight from the strange mid-afternoon darkness. A few brave friends lovingly took down Jesus' lifeless body from the cross. They tenderly, but quickly, washed the blood and dirt from His body knowing they must prepare it for the tomb before the beginning of the Sabbath. They would wrap the body loosely with the intent to return and complete the burial preparations the first of the week. I can almost hear them mournfully whisper to each other the reality that their act of love for the One they worshiped would render them unclean for worship on the Sabbath. Given the cruelty of the afternoon, tenderness must rule the day, and worship be deferred. What irony that the Servant King, proclaimed "the Chosen One" by throngs of Jews a few days before, would now be laid in a borrowed tomb. Where were His followers now? Where were His friends now? In the darkness doubt whispered, "Was everything He told us the truth?" Quickly they laid the body on a wagon and headed for Joseph's tomb.

The streets of downtown Jerusalem were all but deserted after the panic of the mid-day earthquake. Cracked walls and overturned pots littered the streets after everyone fled for shelter or ran from the city for the safety of the surrounding countryside. The shaken temple priests were hurriedly trying to return order to the temple, knowing that the Sabbath was quickly coming upon them; the earthquake had created a considerable mess. Suddenly, they came face to face with the reality that the curtain that kept them from the Holy of Holies was torn, revealing to their view the mercy seat. Fear gripped them as they wondered, "Will we now die from the sight of the mercy seat?" There it set, the "Presence" in plain view as they averted their eyes. But something seemed different now. The torn curtain seemed almost an invitation to them. "Come in to where you could not go before. Set aside the blood of bulls and goats. We can talk now; we can visit together, you and I." The rubble whispered out to them, "Would all of this ever be the same again? Would all of this be necessary anymore?" The Levite wondered, "Could it be the mercy seat was laid in plain view of everyone in the afternoon on a hill outside the city gates?"

A short time later a commotion was being raised near the gates of a spiritual place called Paradise. Ancient saints, kings and beggars had come to this place over centuries to rest in peace and comfort while awaiting the promised freedom work of Messiah, while waiting to enter heaven and worship the LORD in His very presence. Their faith in this promise already counted as their righteousness and, while they had avoided Hades, they yearned for passage to the throne room of the LORD. Recently there were rumors the Messiah had entered the natural world and hopes were high for the final redemption of Paradise. In fact, earlier in the day, many had suddenly vanished from Paradise, and some were now returning with the declaration, "We were sent back to the natural world to bear witness to the testimony of Messiah concerning the Scriptures. We walked in our old bodies and were recognized by many. We saw Messiah lifted on a cross, crucified to death by pagans." The disappointment in their voices brought a quick end to the excitement of the possibility of Paradise's impending redemption. "How much longer must we wait for freedom to enter the LORD's presence?" Jonah declared. "How our hearts burned upon hearing of Messiah's entrance to the natural realm!" Solomon exclaimed.

Their voices were suddenly interrupted by the sentry cry, "Who goes there outside the gate? What manner of Saint are You approaching our blissful abode?" Those inside the gate strained to see the advance of a regal being to the entrance of Paradise. His countenance shown with the light of Heaven's sun, but His eyes were joyful and kind. Shadrach suddenly declared, "Let Him in. I have seen His face before in the fire of a king's furnace centuries ago. He was with my brothers and me in trial and delivered us from harm." The sentry shouted, "Kind Sir, have You come to unlock the gate that for centuries has kept us in Paradise? Do You hold the keys to the stairway to Father's home?"

Walking to the gate, the Regal One replied, "I have no keys to the gate. I am the Key!" And the gates of Paradise began to open at the sound of His voice. He continued, "I declare to all who dwell here that today is the day of your redemption. Today God's blood was laid on the mercy seat, and all your sins washed away. What God could not wholly accept from the blood of bulls and goats has been provided today. Yes, Shadrach, I was the fourth in the fire you saw. I am Ancient of Days, come to do the work of the LORD and restore all to His fellowship. Quickly gather yourselves and prepare to worship, it is but a short trip outside these gates to Heaven's stairway. Find Jacob. He has seen the stairway before and will lead you there."

Slowly an anthem rose from the multitudes in Paradise, and the processional began to pass through the open gates singing, "Faithful and true is the Lamb that redeems us to the Lord our God." Abraham whispered, "God has provided a sacrifice and this time He used His son. Nothing will ever be the same again." Messiah told Jacob, "Move quickly now; I shall join you again after you reach Abba's throne." And then He was gone.

Meanwhile, in the depths of Hades, a hideously loud celebration drowned out the beautiful anthem coming from across the great divide. Such was the devious joy of Hell that few noticed the movement afar in Paradise. Demonic roars and raucous singing had interrupted the usual melancholy suffering upon the news of Messiah's demise. Satan had declared a feast and victory celebration and now led the chorus singing, "I have won, heaven has lost, and the earth and all its inhabitants are mine. I have put ruin to God's plans using those who claimed they knew Him best." Demons and minions drinking steaming gruel shouted, "Hail, Lord Satan! He has won the day." But from the caverns came a whisper, "Something's changed."

A sheepish looking imp entered the party with a whisper to the evil one, "Master, there is someone at the gates of hell demanding to see you." Satan roared, "They must wait. I am celebrating the death of Messiah!" The shivering one replied, "Master, He is very persistent, and He says you must come -- He even commands it. I could not stop Him. He broke open the gate." The devil smashed the back of his hand against the interrupter's face sending him crashing against the rocks. "How dare anyone demand of me anything on the day of my victory! I shall see to this annoyance and dispatch of him quickly. Carry on until I return." Satan rushed to hell's gate with fury shouting, "I'll be damned if anyone will interrupt my triumph. What? It is You! It can't be. We hung You on a tree and mocked You as You died. The face of God turned away from You and all man's futile hope was crushed."

Messiah confidently set aside the broken gate and calmly replied, "Satan, you have finally done it. In your zeal to thwart redemption's plan, you finally killed an innocent man. Your act of open rebellion has accomplished what centuries of sacrifice could not. While the blood of bulls and goats could only cover sin for a season, God's perfect blood was spilled, and its power did not just cover man's sin, but it washed man's sin away for all time. Those that believe this will never die. Now, give Me the keys to this place. You can control hell's gate no more. No longer will men come here because they have to; they will only come here because they choose to." The furious cry from Satan's mouth shook the caverns, "I am doomed! The keys are Yours; I've lost it all. You have claimed the Victor's crown." To which Messiah replied, "Heaven and Hell will never be the same! It is all changed." And then He was gone – along with the keys.

The hues of gray had broken the total darkness above the hills around Jerusalem. Sleepy soldiers huddled close to a small fire that barely revealed the rock walls of Joseph's tomb. The lone temple guard among the Romans continued to engage the soldiers with his recount of the encounter with Jesus at Gethsemane. "There was something different about Him. When our commander demanded if He was the man Jesus, His simple response, 'I Am He,' pounded all of us to the ground. We could not stand until He bid us stand. I fear we, as a people, have perpetrated a great wrong and our priests should have known - should have stopped all this."

The Roman sneered, "He was just another self-proclaimed troublemaker. I saw Him whipped; I saw Him die. He bled like a man and cried like a man - just a man." The temple guard stopped the discourse whispering, "Did you hear the sound – the sound from the tomb." The Roman's response, "Don't be a foolish coward..." interrupted by a crescendo of quaking as the cracking stones tossed in a growing frenzy. There was a flash of light so bright that it cast shadows against the glimmering dawn. Then that voice from the garden in thunder proclaimed, "I Am. I Am alive. I Am He!" The Romans and the temple guard were once again prostrated against the earth, unable to move, unable to speak, unable to see. Messiah stepped from the tomb's entrance with the radiance of the sun glowing from His face. He finished His discourse with, "I Am the Lamb, the Son of Elohim. I Am the surety of God's provision, the treasure of Heaven, the ransom sufficient for all. I Am the first fruits of many to follow, the reality of everlasting life, the gateway to Abba for those who the Father has chosen, for those who answer My call! I have set a fire in Palestine that will burn until it consumes the earth. Today, all has changed; nothing will ever be the same."

From a distance away, women bearing anointing spices in the early morn whispered among themselves, "Mary, did you hear that voice coming from the direction of Joseph's tomb?"

"I heard something," her friend replied. "It sounded much like the Master's voice. Oh, if it could be so! This agony, fear, sorrow, and doubt would all melt away if He would once again speak His peace to us. Wouldn't it be grand? Everything would change – nothing could ever be the same…" Then she heard it, "Mary."

After dreaming my dreams, examining my thoughts and considering the words to the song that follows – knowing that the Kingdom of Christ operates so vastly different than the natural world, I have to consider these four things this Easter.

1. About the time we believe God is dead to our circumstance, He bursts out with new life, hope, wisdom and peace.
2. The road to real glory inevitably passes through the valley of pain and trial.
3. We can always find the keys to Heaven hanging on a cross.
4. The doorway to everlasting life passes through an entrance that closely resembles a tomb.

HE IS ALIVE! HE LIVES IN US! AND WE LIVE IN HIM! All things have changed – nothing will ever be the same!

Song to Consider: "Then Came the Morning" Chris Christian, Bill & Gloria Gaither

Prayer: Lord Jesus, I bow before You and remember all You have done for me. In my heart's eyes, I see an empty cross, an empty tomb, a torn curtain, a living mercy seat. Abba's great love and Your obedient heart have changed everything. Nothing has ever been the same since You left that tomb on Easter's early morning. Abundant life, meaningful life, everlasting life, blooms like the flowers of Spring in the middle of a still broken world. There is light in the darkness; there is hope in despair; there is health in sickness; there is relief in suffering. I have a purpose in the middle of chaos because of what You accomplished through the power of God in three short days nearly two thousand years ago. Change me as You wish. Live in me today so that nothing will ever be the same, Amen.

Loved

"Three things will last forever—faith, hope, and love—and the greatest of these is love.

– Paul the Apostle (1 Corinthians 13:13 NLT)

Why Am I Loved?

A Child Shall Lead Us

Right now, I am thinking about my grandson Micah - yes little Micah Scott Dickerson. He is the newest among us and needs our love and support. It is amazing how someone so small can bring new life and energy into others' lives. He can do little for himself, but he has power over the dynamics of a room when he enters it. My thoughts:

Jesus told His disciples that the Kingdom of God is made up of little children like Micah (Luke 18). He goes on to tell them that the only way to enter God's Kingdom is by becoming little and helpless like Micah is now. God sees us like we see Micah - little and unable to do much for ourselves. He loves us this way. He is always willing to comfort us when we cry, feed us when we are hungry, protect us when we are afraid and, yes, clean us up when we make a mess. In His eyes and His heart, we will always be like Micah regardless of how old, strong, wise and successful we see ourselves. We are the objects of His powerful affection and the focus of His perfect desire. He created us not out of His need (God needs nothing - if He did He would not be God); He created us out of His desire. Just like we do with Micah, He holds on to us - even when we can't (or won't) hold on to Him. Isn't that a reassuring thought? Let's make it our purpose to spend more time being His by resting in His arms and enjoying His presence. He is always willing and always close.

Scriptures:

"Let the children come to me. Don't stop them! For the kingdom of Heaven belongs to those who are like these children" (Matthew 19:14).

"Which of you fathers, if your child asks for a fish, will give him a snake instead? Or if he asks for an egg, will give him a scorpion? If you then, though you are [far less than perfect], know how to give good gifts to your children, how much more will your Father in heaven give His Spirit [abundant life] to those who ask Him!" (Luke 11:13 bracketed words added by the author).

Word for Contemplation:

TRUST - Reliance on the integrity, strength, ability, surety of a person or thing.

We can rely on God's strength, integrity, ability, and surety - but, most of all, we can trust (rely on) His unfailing love.

Where is the Kingdom of Heaven? Can you remember a time when you felt powerless and God intervened on your behalf?

Song to Consider: "The Warrior is a Child" – Twila Paris

Prayer: Father, make me childlike as I trust in You to love me, protect me, keep me, and improve me every day. Abba, I am Yours, and You know how to care for what belongs to you, Amen.

No Greater Love

How do we measure love? In our human condition, it is easy to measure based on "What have you done for me lately." If love is indeed a verb and not a noun, actions, and not feelings as we have discussed before, then the ultimate measure of love could be described as the most effective and greatest action taken for our benefit. If we can identify this action, then we should be able to rest assured in the arms of love.

Jesus said in John 15:13, "Greater love has no one than this: to lay down one's life for one's friends." He backed this up when He gave Himself to be punished and put to death in our place. Hear me when I say, If God never did another thing for us in this life, He has done all love requires for our sake. We may go through tough places and have to endure trouble because of the state of this broken world, but we must never question the love of God. To take this concept even further, Romans 5:7-8 tell us, "Very rarely will anyone die for a righteous person, though for a good person [or a friend] someone might possibly dare to die. But God demonstrates his own love for us in this: While we were still sinners, Christ died for us."

Do we sulk when we believe we are in need? Do we complain to God when we feel lonely or unloved? Look back to the cross and remember that Jesus took our punishment there. He, though perfect, laid down His life for all of us who were imperfect. Let's not cop to the "what have you done for me lately" attitude with God. He has nothing left to prove. With grateful hearts, let's go to Him in the good times and the bad times. Because of His great love, the best for us is always yet to come.

My Song: The Best of Your Love – Ken Dickerson

Sin's prison was dark,
And strong were my chains.
The guilt in my heart,
Left no hope to ease my pain.
Then Jesus came down,
In love brought the keys.

He opened the bars,
Broke my chains and set me free.

You broke open Your heart
And You poured out the treasure of Heaven.
The very best of Your love
Got hung on a rugged tree.
I know a righteous man died
To make sure that my sins were forgiven.
Lord, it took the best of Your love
To reach down and rescue me.
God, You counted the cost
When You knew I was lost.
Heaven's ransom was raised,
A broken world could be saved.

Prayer: Father, You have done all love requires for me. Help me to never question how much You love me. Give me a grateful heart knowing that I will dwell in Your presence forever because of the best of Your love. Create in me this same kind of love that acts on behalf of others so they can experience Your gracious and loving heart. For Jesus' sake, Amen.

Caught Between Mercy and Grace

Have you ever really thought about the difference between mercy and grace? We could have long, theological discussions about all the implications of these terms, but to me mercy is all about not receiving what we deserve, and grace is all about getting much more than we deserve. God's mercy worked through Jesus by washing away our sins and saving us from eternal separation from God. This work is important because we all have failed to live up to the standard of God's perfection. We are less than perfect by nature, and we are less than perfect by choice. By God's love and His great mercy our sins are washed away and through Jesus' sacrifice the wages of our sins were put upon Him on the cross. Our sins are washed away, forgiven and forgotten. He spared us the wages of a second death and the suffering of eternal separation from God the Father. Whew! I am glad I don't get what I deserve.

Now grace is the cool part of God's benefits. Grace takes its form in all the good things we receive from the Father that we don't deserve. Things like an eternal home, an eternal family, abundant life, everlasting life, hope, joy, peace, righteousness, and the power to become the children of God. Grace is God's goodness that follows us all the days of our lives and surrounds us with His perfect care. Grace is the working of His Spirit in us to make us more loving, gentle, kind, and grace gives us more self-control while assuring us that we are never alone. Grace is the love we share with each other, our friends, and, yes, our not-so-friends. Grace is the power to become all that Abba created us to be. Grace is God always calling us closer to Him. Amazing, unending and unbounded grace is ours for the asking. Take time every day to ask for grace. I promise you will always get it, and many times it will be overflowing beyond what we can imagine.

"I do not at all understand the mystery of grace - only that it meets us where we are but does not leave us where it found us."

–Anne Lamott

Scriptures:

"For you know the *grace* of our Lord Jesus Christ that though he was rich, yet for your sake he became poor, so that you through his poverty you might become rich" (2 Corinthians 8:9). "At one time we too were foolish, disobedient, deceived and enslaved by all kinds of passions and pleasures. We lived in malice and envy, being hated and hating one another. But when the kindness and love of God our Savior appeared, he saved us, not because of righteous things we had done, but because of his mercy. He saved us through the washing of rebirth and renewal by the Holy Spirit, he poured out on us generously through Jesus Christ our Savior, so that, having been justified by his grace, we might become heirs having the hope of eternal life" (Titus 3:3-7).

Can you remember times when you have received better than you deserved? How did you feel?

Song to Consider: "Grace" - Tonic-Sol-Fa

My Song: Your Name Is Mercy

Your name is Mercy, Father I belong to you.
Your grace has found me, and Your love has made me new.
I was nothing without You, but I'm priceless because of You.
Your name is Mercy; I needed mercy,
Your name is Mercy, Father, I belong to You.

It was not for any good that I have done.
It was not for any kindness that I ever showed to You.
I was wandering in the darkness with no place to call my home.
Then You found me; Your grace has found me.

Your name is Mercy, Father, I belong to You.
Your grace has found me, and Your love has made me new.
I was nothing without You, but I'm priceless because of You.
Your name is Mercy; I needed mercy,
Your name is Mercy, Father, I belong to you.

Prayer: Abba, I am so grateful that Your wonderful grace has found me. You are great, You are kind, and You are good all the time. Help me not to hang on to grace, but to pass it on every chance I get. Your grace is the power that really can change me, my family, my friends, and, yes, the world, Amen.

Christ seize us by the power of Your great affection every day.

Uniquely Familiar

It has always intrigued me how Jesus could simultaneously be so compelling and revolting in the same circumstances. He was concurrently found compassionate to the humble and conspiring to the haughty. The subjects of His gracious actions praised Him while, at the same time, raised-eyebrow spectators condemned Him. The unrighteous repented in response to His kindness while the perceived righteous plotted evil against Him. While this enigma might confound the wisdom of the world, we should not be surprised at it, and we should even expect this reaction to our lives as we follow the Divine Rabbi carpenter from Nazareth. We need to be *uniquely familiar* to the world around us. Our lives need to be familiar enough that those looking for hope see possibility, yet we need to be unique enough to make the sinner uncomfortable to practice in our presence. Like applying salt to wounds, our lives should present the painful promise of healing.

How can we be in this world without being of this world? How can we love sinners and hate sin? How can we live in righteousness while embracing the unrighteous with the Father's unbounded love? There are keys to this enigma that we can make a part of our lives. They are transparency, humility, charity, and truth.

Jesus lived a totally transparent life. Everything He said was God's Word, and everything He did was God's will. He lived life to honor His Father, and His vision and mission were consistent with God's plan that was already revealed in Scripture. Soon after Jesus healed the cripple by the Bethesda pool, He told the religious crowd questioning His work on the Sabbath, "I tell you the truth, the Son can do nothing by himself. He does only what He sees the Father doing. Whatever the Father does, the Son also does. For the Father loves the Son and shows him everything he is doing. In fact, the Father will show him how to do even greater works than healing this man. Then you will truly be astonished" (John 5:19-20). In John 14, Jesus told Thomas and Philip, "The words I speak are not my own, but my Father, who lives in me does his work through me."

Why are we chosen? Is it not that we have a purpose to do God's will and speak God's truth? We should live our lives in transparency with no hidden agenda or purpose other than to exalt and honor Jesus. People should see Jesus in us and hear Jesus through us and then, they will have a decision to make. Some will draw near while others will run away. Some will repent while others will persecute. Some will be grateful, and others will be offended. It's not our purpose to manage outcomes – it is our purpose to plant a seed and to water the seed and pray for the increase. It is our purpose to show forth the praise of the One who has called us out of darkness into light and out of death and into life. Since Eden, man has been hiding, so, the world finds transparency both troubling and frightening. It is hard for carnal men to embrace life with glass walls and no secret places. The thought of this exposure rubs most people the wrong way. But truth cries out, "You cannot hide from God, who knows all, sees all, and is everywhere at all times." However, the carnal man, still stumbles to the bushes and hides in the dark.

Jesus embraced humility and humbled himself. He left the splendor of heaven for the earth to live with us. He clothed Himself with the rags of humanity to suffer with us. He laid aside immortality to die for us trusting in His Father to raise Him back to life. The Apostle Paul, speaking to the Philippians, says, "Let this mind be in you, which was also in Christ Jesus: who, being in the form of God, thought it not robbery to be equal with God: but made himself of no reputation, and took upon him the form of a servant, and was made in the likeness of men: and being found in fashion as a man, he humbled himself, and became obedient unto death, even the death of the cross" (Philippians 2:5-8).

True followers of Jesus understand we are called to lay down our lives, our influence, our riches, our credit, and our comfort for the benefit of a broken, hostile, ungrateful, and dying world. While our salvation is freely given, our service exacts a great price. Ridicule, scorn, misunderstanding, and suspicion may follow us frequently. We are a peculiar people because we live life differently, not for ourselves but for our Christ and any others He may choose to touch through us - some of them lovely, some not so lovely, some downright mean.

Jesus loved deeply. Matthew 9 tells us, "Jesus traveled through all the towns and villages of that area, teaching in the synagogues and announcing the Good News about the Kingdom. And he healed every kind of disease and illness. When he saw the crowds, *he had compassion on them* because they were confused and helpless, like sheep without a shepherd." I love Brennan Manning's words about this kind of compassion.

> "Jesus says to your heart and mine; don't ever be so foolish in measuring my compassion for you regarding your compassion for one another. Don't ever be so silly as to compare your thin, pallid, moody, depending on smooth circumstances, human compassion with mine for I am God as well as man." When you read in the gospel that Jesus was moved with compassion it is saying his gut was wrenched; his heart torn open; the most vulnerable part of his being laid bare. The ground of all beings shook, the source of all life trembled, the heart of all love burst open, and the unfathomable depth of his relentless tenderness was laid bare. Your Christian life and mine don't make any sense unless in the depth of our beings we believe that Jesus not only knows what hurts us, but knowing, seeks us out, whatever our poverty, whatever our pain, his plea to his people is, "Come now wounded, frightened, angry, lonely, empty and I'll meet you where you live, and I'll love you as you are, not as you should be. Because you're never going be as you should be" (Brennan Manning on God's Love, https://youtu.be/0dMwu1rhTCQ.

Can we believe in a compassionate love like this? Can we live a compassionate love like this? Can we meet others where they are? This love can change lives. This kind of love has changed the world and is changing the world. This love is more than a feeling; it is action, it is energy, it is life, it is the power of God. Oh what love the Father has given to us that we can become His children and invite others to His family!

Jesus always spoke the truth. Just before His death Jesus offered this prayer as recorded in John:

> "*Make them holy by your truth; teach them your word, which is truth.* Just as you sent me into the world, I am sending them into the world. And I give myself as a holy sacrifice for them so they can be made holy by your truth. I am praying not only for these disciples *but also for all who will ever believe in me through their message. I pray that they will all be one, just as you and I are one—as you are in me, Father, and I am* in you. And *may they be in us so that the world will believe you sent me.* I have given them the glory you gave me, so they may be one as we are one. I am in them, and you are in me. May they experience such perfect unity that the world will know that you sent me and that you love them as much as you love me. Father, I want these whom you have given me to be with me where I am. Then they can see all the glory you gave me because you loved me even before the world began! O righteous Father, the world doesn't know you, but I do; and these disciples know you sent me. I have revealed you to them, and I will continue to do so. Then your love for me will be in them, and I will be in them" (John 17: 17-26 emphasis added).

Here is the truth, the truth that will redeem every fallen man, crush the fear of death, and open the door of everlasting life: God created us for His pleasure and purpose. He is Lord of all. Jesus is the only way to God. He is the only cure for a deceitful, self-centered heart. There is no purpose to life apart from Him. He will live inside of us if we ask Him to and is gathering an everlasting family to live with Him forever.

After this truth, all else is trivial at best. The energies expended in pursuit of material things, and worldly pleasures, will lay exhausted in a tomb. All of mans' games, schemes, power hungry dreams, riches, and honors will be consumed by fire. Christ in us and us in Christ is all that will endure. The world cannot escape this truth; this truth so hard to accept when a man is the center of his world. This truth brings hope to the hopeless but judgment to those who think they have it all. When we carry this truth in us, we simultaneously heal and open wounds.

The enigma is that the foundation stone of all creation's purpose is a stumbling block to those who try and skip over it. The things the world can see, feel, touch, and smell will all pass away. The things embraced with grateful and faithful hearts, though invisible to our eyes, are the things that will last forever. This truth is hard for a broken, self-centered world to grab. Pray that eyes and hearts are opened by the Spirit of truth. Live transparently, walk humbly, love deeply, and tell the truth. Live in a manner that the world sees as *uniquely familiar*. Many will take notice, and some will be radically changed.

Song to Consider: "In Christ Alone" – Michael English

Prayer: My Gracious Father, help me live in a manner that brings hope to the hopeless yet makes the world uncomfortable with their sin. Let me stand exposed in a manner that reveals the work You are doing to change me and my heart, and make me one of Your dearly loved children -- a child that looks like You, talks like You, and acts like You. Give me Your capacity for compassion that deeply loves and longs for mercy. Jesus, help me always tell the truth that You alone are God – the cure for sin and the hope for sinners. Make me uniquely familiar to those who You lead into my pathway – those who are chosen to encounter Your glory and love. For Your Kingdom's cause, Amen.

Living Prepared to Love

Closer than Close

I want to encourage you about the nearness of God. Jesus is Emmanuel "God with Us". In the days of the Old Testament, man could not look upon God's face and live. When Moses returned with the commandments from the top of Mt. Sinai, his face glowed like a blinding light having viewed only Jehovah's shadow. Men died for touching or mishandling the Ark of the Covenant where God's glory sat. Elohim was best encountered with a bowed head and at a good distance.

When Jesus came to earth, His disciples and thousands of others got to look on the face of God and saw in it, not terror and death, but compassion and hopefulness. No longer would God hold Himself at arm's length because of our sorry, sinful state. He sent Jesus to do something about it. Jesus came on the human scene as the Father's embrace of our condition. He came as the Father's declaration of love. Jesus became the solution to the distance between Jehovah and us. Finally, God reached down and hugged all of us (mankind).

After Jesus settled our account and solved our sorry state at Calvary; after He obliterated the power of death and hell with His resurrection; He returned in His glorified body to heaven and His rightful place at the Father's side. But He left with a promise to those who had walked with Him on earth, to those He had chosen. He promised to send His Spirit (the life of His mind and His heart) to not only dwell with them, but to dwell in them. This promise is still valid to us today: His life, His power, His love, His mind inside of us. As His dearly loved children, we need not search for God anywhere beyond ourselves. Through Jesus, God came near to us and, through His Spirit, God comes to live inside of us.

God's transcendence allows Him simultaneously to fill the biggest void of space and the smallest corner of our heart. The great twentieth-century pastor and author A. W. Tozer , in his book, *The Pursuit of God,* says: "We need never to shout across the spaces to an absent God. He is nearer than our own soul, closer than our most secret thoughts" (page 51).

In Acts 17, the Apostle Paul quoted the Cretan poet Epimenides to the Athenians saying, "In Him we live, and move, and have our being." (I like to translate our being as our significance). The Creator has come to dwell in us. We, though once wretched and poor are rich, though once weak and down-trodden, are strong, though once held at arm's length, now are made one with the Creator through a supernatural embrace by His Holy Spirit. The Holy Spirit surrounds us with God's presence and fills up every part of us with Him as we surrender.

In the famous gospel song, "How Big is God?" composer Stuart Hamblin wrote: "God is big enough to fill the mighty universe, yet small enough to live within our heart."

We may, at times, envy the original disciples privilege to walk with Jesus, talk with Jesus, listen to Him teach, and see His face while here on earth. They were very fortunate that He lived with them. However, after the years of relationship, the miracles, the teaching, when things got tough, they were nowhere to be found. One betrayed Him, one denied Him, while the rest went cowering in fear for their lives. Even after seeing Him in His resurrected body, they were bewildered when He returned to Heaven.

About fifty days later, Jesus returned to them by way of His Spirit at Pentecost. He returned not just to live with them, but also to live in them. This same group spread His Good News with such authority and courage that they changed the world. Two thousand years later, we have the same opportunity as they did: to allow Him to live in us so we, too, can change our world.

Scriptures

Acts 1: 1-18

Acts 17:28

Do you remember a time when God showed up when you called? Do you remember a time when God worked through you to make peace, give grace or work mercy? How did it feel?

Song to Consider: "He's as Close as the Mention of His Name"

Prayer: Holy Spirit of God, I invite you to fill me with Your mind, Your power and Your love. I present myself as Your dwelling place and give thanks that You choose to dwell in me. Stay closer than my thoughts, closer than my breath, closer than my soul. Empower me to change my world, Amen.

Desperate Saints/Desperate Sinners

"Two men went up to the house of God to pray. One of them was a proud religious law-keeper. The other was a man who gathered taxes. The proud religious law-keeper stood and prayed to himself like this, 'God, I thank You that I am not like other men. I am not like those who steal. I am not like those who do things that are wrong. I am not like those who do sex sins. I am not even like this tax-gatherer. I go without food two times a week so I can pray better. I give one-tenth part of the money I earn.' But the man who gathered taxes stood a long way off. He would not even lift his eyes to heaven. But he hit himself on his chest and said, 'God, have mercy on me! I am a sinner.' *I tell you, this man went back to his house forgiven, and not the other man*" (Luke 18:10-14 emphasis added).

I spent Sunday in church with over two hundred addicts. It has been a long time since I felt the power of God like heavy fog in a room. This power was awesome, rich and humbling. These folks were desperate for change. These folks were desperate for God. When hundreds of desperate saints and sinners cry out to God in worship, they always get the benefit of His best ear. We sang, "There is power in the name of Jesus – to break every chain, break every chain, break every chain." My best Sunday attitude quickly changed to desperation too. You see, we are all desperate people living in a desperate world and living a life that dangles by a thin silver thread so easily broken. Some of us don't realize how desperate we are. This self-centered, self-idolizing culture of modern western civilization constantly shouts in our ears, "You are the masters of your domain, the means to the end and the end to the means." The American gospel of exceptionalism flies in the face of the message of Christ that proclaims, "The heart is deceitful and desperately wicked – few can realize it" and "The best we have to offer God is like filthy rags." Our so-called rugged individualism and independent streak have become at odds with the Lordship of Christ. Our infatuation with things we can see, feel, touch, smell, and consume robs us of our ability to experience the eternal reality of eternal things – the really real things that last forever like faith, hope, love, generosity, kindness, self-control and peace.

We worship God in our air-conditioned sanctuaries, sitting on our cushioned pews, cheering from the stands, but never really taking our cross and entering the battle. We close our eyes and pray to a God, wearing a butler's suit, to bring us what we need to eat, drink and be merry. We throw our coins in the offering with no regard for the wages of our self-centeredness or the terrible cost to redeem us. Many in our world go through life stumbling among the manna and the quail while never acknowledging the One who gives it, that is, until the silver thread breaks. Then, lying battered and scarred at the bottom of the heap, they lift their eyes to find the eyes of kindness looking down and the hands of mercy reaching down for them so desperate for the kindness that leads to repentance.

We do better when we are desperate. The power of the cry, "Have mercy on me, Lord!" brings dramatic and lasting change. Desperation catches the attention of the compassionate One. It moves Him to acts of love and salvation and healing and mercy. I want to become desperate again. Desperate for His presence, desperate to hear His voice, desperate to see His power, desperate to receive His provision, desperate for freedom from this unholy independent streak that spreads like a communicable disease, poisoning, dividing and conquering us until we stand for only what's mine and not what's ours in Christ. I want to be desperate to worship like my Faith Farm friends across the bridge in Boynton Beach, desperate to walk through the thick presence of God's holiness in the middle of desperate lives. I want to live constantly reminded that He is all we have – but He is all we need. I want to have the attention of God's best ear.

Before I left Boynton Beach, I got the names of several of the folks I met so that I might remember them before Abba's throne. On Tuesday morning as I prayed, the Lord spoke to me concerning their desperate situations. As He spoke these words to my heart, I could see the faces of many children singing, "There is power in the name of Jesus to break every chain, break every chain, break every chain." This song will be in my spirit for a long, long time. Some of those children I saw had the faces of my grandsons.

These words are prophetic words for my friends across the bridge in Boynton Beach. I know some of you will read this devotional. Stay desperate my friends. You have the Father's full attention. He says:

I have heard your desperate cries and tell you, if you will give Me all your heart, and follow after Me with all your mind and strength, I will restore to you all that was stolen, all that has been lost, and all that was carelessly given away in such great measure that you can feed yourself and share all I have restored with others who find they are as desperate for mercy as you have realized yourself to be.

Song: "My Highest Praise" – Ken Dickerson

More than a song Lord,
More than a sweet embrace.
All that I have I lay in worship at Your feet.
My heart beats, "Yes, Lord."
I choose the path down which You lead.
Quick to take up my cross and follow You alone.
A contrite spirit finds strength in doing things Your way.
Because my highest form of praise.
No greater gift I'll ever raise.
I know my highest form of praise is to surrender.

I surrender all; I surrender all.
All to Jesus my wondrous Savior.
I surrender, I surrender all.

Blessings, and stay desperate my friends.

Prayer: Jesus, Savior, keep me always desperate for You. Give me an insatiable hunger and thirst for You, Your word, and Your ways. Pour over me, Holy one. For mercy's sake come fill me up, until all I am brings glory to Your wondrous love and Your name Almighty God. I bring my praise Almighty God, Amen.

Love Is Something You Do

What is love? This powerful force is one of the most over-hyped and misunderstood concepts to confront mankind. What is the longing in man's heart? For what is he looking?

In the song, "Flaws," as performed by Bastille, Daniel Smith wrote about a hole in his soul, asking who could fill the hole he could not fill.

If love is what the world needs now, if love is the only thing that can fill the hole in my soul, it is important that I have a true understanding of what love is. Ever since Eden, when Adam and Eve tore this hole in their souls, men and women have tried to fill it with all sorts of love impersonations and love substitutes, and the desperate search still goes on for love. A quick summary of modern music reveals titles and statements like, "you've lost that lovin' feeling" or "love me tender" or "looking for love in all the wrong places." If the truth is known, the Scripture reveals that love is not a feeling and does not necessarily have to be tender. Perhaps the ever-elusive love feeling comes from a misconception that love is a noun when love is a verb. True love, God's love, is action. Love may elicit feelings as a result of its action, but the reality is that love does not feel – it acts. Love is a decision to assign worth and act on that decision. "For God so loved the world _He gave..._" Compassion is not love, compassion can lead to love, but it does not necessarily do so. If I see the street beggar, I can have compassion but until I act on behalf of his wellbeing, I have not loved him. The receipt of love, though fulfilling, can never bring the joy that acting out love brings. Hence the words of the Divine Rabbi, "It is more blessed to give than receive." The joy we receive as recipients of God's powerful, divine affection is nothing compared to the joy that God the Father's heart feels at the result of His great act of love. He commanded the Treasure of Heaven (Jesus, God the Son) to be humbled and made flesh and to suffer and die so that man, who He created in His image and who He breathed His eternal life into, could be restored to the right standing man enjoyed with the Creator in Eden. When Jesus declared to God the Father, "It is finished," the Creator's joyous rapture thundered through all of Heaven and created an earthquake that ripped the veil of the temple down the middle, exposing His holiness to all who would dare look in faith to the new, living seat of mercy. Jesus proved He knew how to do love.

Physical attraction may lead to love, but it has just as great a chance of leading to heartache. If lust is the currency of a relationship, then what holds the relationship when all that is left are wrinkles, gray hair, failing eyes, and bodies losing the struggle against gravity? This physical attraction may perpetuate the species, but it will not fill the hole in man's soul. Sexual transactions may bring short term satisfaction but, left to their own, do not fulfill the requirements of long-term covenant.

I want to share with you a brief synopsis of real love from Rick Warren's website, *Daily Hope*. Dr. Warren tells us:

> "Dear children, let us stop just saying we love each other; **let us really show it by our actions.**" (1 John 3:18 NLT)

> Love is more than attraction and more than arousal. It's also more than sentimentality, like so many of today's songs suggest. By this standard, **is love dead when the emotion is gone? No, not at all. Because love is an action; love is a behavior.**

> Over and over again in the Bible, God commands us to love each other. And **you can't command an emotion.** If I told you, "Be sad!" you couldn't be sad on cue. Just like an actor, you can fake it, but **you're not wired for your emotions to change on command.** Have you ever told a little kid, "Be happy!" *"I'm trying, daddy!"*

> If love were just an emotion, then God couldn't command it. But love is something you do. It can produce emotion, but love is an action

> The Bible says, "... Let us stop just saying we love each other; let us really show it by our actions." (1 John 3:18, NLT) We can talk a good act: 'I love people.' But do we really love them? Do you really love them? Our love is revealed in how we act toward them. (http://pastorrick.com/devotional/english/love-is-an-action_844)

Paul gives a great accounting of what love is and what love is not; what love does and does not do. Let's look closely at I Corinthians 13, verses 4-8, according to my personal translation:

Love acts out patience; love passes out kindness, love creates great esteem, but does not brag about its success. Love honors the objects of its affection and lays down its interests for their well-being. Love takes no offense and wastes no time holding angry grudges. Love accomplishes goodness by always telling the truth with the knowledge that the truth brings freedom and reconciliation to all who learn it well. Love stands up for the benefit of others, always trusting that the seed it sows will grow joy and hope in their lives. ***Love never gives up and never gives in - continually acting on the worth it has assigned.***

Jesus says, "If you love Me, you will do what I ask you to do." Remember, this is a command to act, not feel. We must love Him (act out obedience) with all our being. We must act out love toward ourselves, knowing the worth He assigns us; we must act out love to one another (those in our natural and faith families); we must act out love to our neighbors; we must act out love to our enemies.

Have we forsaken relationships because we are offended? That's not love. Have we abandoned help to others because it takes them too long to change? That's not love. Have we elevated our self-interests above the interests of our spouses, children, parents, fellow workers, siblings, and neighbors? That's not love. Have we demeaned ourselves and attested we are worthless when God the Father paid all of Heaven's treasure to redeem us and reconcile us to Himself? That's not love. Have we hoarded resources that could bring grace, generosity and mercy to those around us in need or great trouble? That's not love.

For God so loved the world, ***He gave...*** That's love. Acts of honor, acts of grace, acts of generosity, acts of kindness, acts of patience, acts of tenderness, acts of mercy -- these acts are what fill the hole in our soul. What can we do today to act out love? When we figure this out then, "our world will be a better place" and we will receive *the joy of doing love* to fill the hole in our soul because it is more blessed to give love than to receive love.

Song to Consider: "The Love of God" – Rich Mullins

Prayer: Father, in Heaven, let me know the joy of doing love. Empower me to act out forgiveness, kindness, mercy, generosity, and encouragement to all I find in my pathway today. Help me reconcile with others, as You reconciled with me, by laying down my interests so that they may come to know the reckless, raging fury of Your love. Fill the hole in my soul with opportunities to do love. The kind of love that lasts, the kind of love that heals, the kind of love that sows hope and joy in those hungry and thirsty for grace. Help me abandon my search for elusive sentiments and feelings and embrace the hard work of love – just like You did for my sake, Amen.

Wholly Holy

The Christmas song "O Holy Night" talks about a night like no other night. It talks about a night set aside by God to introduce His Son, in human form, and to begin a violent plan to overtake a dark world with His everlasting Kingdom. Two thousand years later we, His chosen children, remain a part of this plan. For those of us who are struggling to obtain holiness, I want to consider a different slant on holiness. Hopefully, this will make our struggle for holiness seem a little more hopeful.

When the heavens opened, and he saw the Lord, Isaiah spoke of the seraphim calling out, "Holy, Holy, Holy is the Lord God Almighty." He knew he was in a very special place, viewing a very special person. He was in a place like no other, seeing someone like no other. Much like we would exclaim today, "This is a really, really, really special place" or "He is really, really, really special," these beings are adding emphasis to the fact that the Lord God Almighty is like no other, set apart and really, really, really special.

We are not yet perfect, so we cannot lay claim to being holy, holy, holy. However, we are made righteous by God's Son, and we are being made holy. We mistakenly pursue holiness as if it were perfection when our holiness simply means to be set apart for a special purpose. In other words, we are instruments of praise and worship and our quest should be directed at becoming a useful and purposeful instrument.

"But you are a chosen people, a royal priesthood, a _holy n_ation, _God's special possession_, that you may declare the praises of him who called you out of darkness into his wonderful light" (1 Peter 2:9 emphasis added). Peter is declaring we are God's special people set apart for His service and His pleasure. How then do we obtain holiness – special instruments that are useful to our LORD? Here is what I believe is readily obtainable to us.

"Therefore, as God's chosen people, _holy_ and dearly loved, clothe yourselves with compassion, kindness, humility, gentleness and patience" (Colossians 3:12). Let's take our focus off perfection, for God will perfect us eventually. Let's focus on compassion, kindness, humility, gentleness, and patience. These are most obtainable as we choose to live our life close to the One who is Holy, Holy, Holy. If we can master these, I promise you we will be holy. That is beautifully useful instruments, specially equipped for God's purposes and praise. There is no grander goal, no higher calling, or greater fulfillment. This purpose is where joy and peace and hope abide. This purpose fulfills who our good Father says we are.

Song to Consider: "Good, Good Father" – Pat Barret/Anthony Brown

Prayer: My gracious Father and Glorious LORD, while my perfection is not yet obtainable, You have made me righteous in Christ, and I can be holy. While I am not yet perfect, I am Yours - set apart for Your pleasure, Your use, and Your praise. Make Yourself famous through me today as I learn from You compassion, kindness, humility, gentleness and patience. For Jesus' sake and Your Kingdom's cause, Amen.

Great Expectations

Let's consider the following scriptures.

"Blessed are you when people insult you, persecute you and falsely say all kinds of evil against you because of me. *Rejoice and be glad,* because great is your reward in heaven ... " (Matthew 5:11-12 emphasis added).

"*Carry each other's burdens,* and in this way you will fulfill the law of Christ. If anyone thinks they are something when they are not, they deceive themselves. Each one should test their own actions. Then they can take pride in themselves alone, *without comparing themselves to someone else,* ⁵for each one should carry their own load" (Galatians 6:2-5 emphasis added).

"*There is only one Lawgiver and Judge,* the one who is able to save and destroy. But you—*who are you to judge your neighbor?*" (James 4:12 emphasis added).

I think about what Jesus must have thought, being God, when He looked at all the multitudes just before He blessed the small lunch and multiplied it over 5,000 times to feed them when they were hungry. He knew each heart and mind, and He certainly knew who was there with a genuine hunger for righteousness and who was there only for the miracles. *Those wanting the free show far outnumbered the genuine believers, but He fed them all.*

I think about what Jesus must have thought, being God, when He looked out on the hillside at everyone watching Him as He hung on a cross. Being God, *He knew the ones who would follow, and He also knew how many, many more would ultimately reject all He offered. But, He went ahead and died for them all.*

Jesus had great expectations. He had expectations for a Kingdom that would change the course of history. He had expectations for redemption, restoration, eternal life. He had expectations for His father that, as painful as the moment was, Father knew what He was doing.

What are our expectations concerning the people we touch each day? What are our expectations for each other? Are we bound and determined that we will conform others to our expectations and make them into someone like our image? There is only One with the power to change hearts and minds and behaviors, and it is Jesus. He alone has the power to conform people into His image. We cannot conform each other into our image. We are different and yet the same. We all are plagued by sin and need redemption. We all have our unique faults that give us the greatest challenges. We have false expectations, believing that we can expect one another to become ideal in each other's minds.

The thing is, God thinks this is grand -- that is, that we are all so different. Our continuous long-term process of sanctification for His purposes rubs on each other and brings about opportunities for growth. *We are called to love, not change, one another.* If our great expectations are in Christ alone, then we will have the freedom to love without condition, believing that change will come from God. If our great expectations remain in each other, we will live in constant disappointment with each other's inability to conform to what we think is ideal. We will get wounded instead of getting sharpened by our God-ordained interactions. If God is sovereign, then we must believe we are in the right time, the right place and the right circumstance.

Our purpose is to be cups from which others can drink God's Spirit and the platters from which they can eat God's life. This purpose makes us ripe for abuse. We must come to grips with this, or we will shrink from our calling. That calling is, to be salt and light to the world around us, an offering poured out for God's honor and God's glory. This offering is a painful calling, and the stakes are high, but it has great reward. Can we embrace the pain of living to be broken and spilled out to receive the Father's "Well done" and our Lord Jesus' radiant smile?

Song to Consider: "Follow Close to Me"

Prayer: Lord Jesus, forgive me for all my expectations in anything or anyone but You. Grant to me a resilient heart that is unafraid to love, unafraid to give and unafraid to live in proximity to those You have placed in my life. Help me to avoid the trap of trying to conform others to my expectations and leave the process and outcomes of change to

Your perfect plan. Let me walk in joy and peace with those around me knowing You to be both sovereign and merciful to all, Amen.

Attitude of Gratitude

Give thanks with a grateful heart. Give thanks that we have each other. Give thanks that we are not alone. Give thanks for provision, abundance and freedom. We are so blessed, and we are so loved. Give thanks to someone who touches your life with grace and richness.

I am thankful for all of you. I am thankful for the difference you make in my life and the joy and hope you bring to me. Every one of you has purpose and significance. Let's look for ways to bless each other as we live out life together.

When we practice and develop an attitude of gratitude, it accrues to our great benefit. The first step is to be grateful to God. Psalm 118:1 says, "Give thanks to the Lord, for he is good, his love endures forever." Our gratitude is built on this primise. We are grateful because _He is good and His love endures forever._ Every blessing of life flows from God's goodness and love. While it is important to be thankful for all we receive from Him, it is _more important to be thankful for Him._ He is life, He is joy, He is peace, He is hope, and He is provision.

It is important that we express thanks to people. _God ministers most all things that are really important to us through other people._ A. W. Tozer tells us, "Being grateful to God's servants is to be grateful to God and... _we thank God when we thank His people."_ As I shared in a Thanksgiving email, "We do not live alone." We all have people in our lives that make us richer in many things other than money - people that make us wiser, more productive, more generous and, yes, more grateful.

There is a chart of 31 benefits an attitude of gratitude can bring from research done by Amit Aman (google it). Studies show that gratitude not only can be deliberately cultivated, but can increase levels of well-being and happiness among those who do cultivate it. Also, grateful thinking—and especially expression of it to others—is associated with increased levels of energy, optimism and empathy.

Finally, in our culture, it is important for us to realize and be grateful for how much we receive. Our poor in America live like kings compared to 80% of the rest of the world. I believe we need to realize when we see our cup half empty, that it's not the level of what is in our cup, but the size of our cup for which we should be grateful. In America, we have all been given large cups.

Let's resolve to take the point of view that our God can bring good out of all things and bring richness forth from all people. Romans 8 reminds us that all things work together for our good. Let's be those who agree with the French novelist Alphonse Karr, who stated, "Some people grumble that roses have thorns; I am grateful that thorns have roses."

Song to Consider: "For the Beauty of the Earth" - Pierpoint

My Song: "Jesus Lord of All"

With my heart full of thanks, and
My mouth full of praise,
I lift my voice to the Ancient of Days;
To the Mighty God, to the Mighty God,
Jesus Lord of all.
To the Mighty God, to the Mighty God,
Jesus Lord of all.

Holy, Holy, God Almighty,
Full of grace and truth.
Holy, Holy, God Almighty,
Beautiful Saviour, You are.
Holy, Holy, God Almighty,
Full of grace and truth.
Holy, Holy, God Almighty,
Beautiful Saviour, You are – You are!

(Bridge)
Nothing can separate us from His abiding love.
Not the depth of the sea, or the dark of the night,
He is there – He is there!

With my heart full of thanks, and
My mouth full of praise,

I lift my voice to the Ancient of Days;
To the Mighty God, to the Mighty God,
Jesus Lord of all.
To the Mighty God, to the Mighty God,
Jesus Lord of all.

Prayer: Father, give me more chances to practice an attitude of gratitude. I thank You for giving Yourself to me by the life of Your Spirit that dwells in me and works through me. Create in me a grateful heart that focuses on the good in all people and the good in all You have created for my benefit. Let me start and finish every day with thankfulness and let me put into action that thankfulness as I live with others. In Jesus' name, Amen.

Making God Smile

It was a blessing to see Billy Graham, on his 95th birthday, do an interview on a nationally televised program, _My Hope for America._ What a privilege it has been to live in a time when the Good News has been spread across the world, and in no small part because of great preachers like Rev. Graham. Throughout my life, I have often dreamed of doing great things for God. When I was young, I would dream about what it would be like to preach to 10,000 people at a time or sing in large churches. I wanted to be significant in the Kingdom - to do big things for God, make Him proud, make Him famous...

I had a conversation with one of my Christian buddies the other day, a man who has done some big things in business and churches during his life. He has taken a step back from the big things and was wondering with me: _What does God consider big in His Kingdom? What really pleases God?_

We talked some about creation. If we take a quick look back at the creation story in Genesis, we can get a glimpse of what pleases God most. In Genesis 1:3-25, we get the account of the remarkable creative power of God as He spoke into existence the universe, the stars, the planets, the moon, the earth, the plants, the sea, the dry ground, and the animals with just the power of His words. "And God said" again and again, and it happened. It was so grand that God looked and declared it all "good." Listen, when God says it's good, it is excellent beyond compare. After all, He's God. What more could be done to glorify His great creativity?

In verse 26, we see that God the Father turned to the Son and the Spirit and exclaimed, "Let us make man in Our likeness so he can rule over all this grandeur." How God accomplished this tells a beautiful story of His care and His heart and what motivates His great love. Verse 7 of Chapter 2 is brief but compelling. Instead of speaking man into existence, as He had done with the rest of His vast creation, He bent down and, with His hands, He formed the dust of the earth into a temple that resembled Himself. Then, without a word, He bent down and kissed man, breathing into Adam the very breath of God -- His breath, His life, His mind, His heart. Listen closely family: we are made different from the rest of creation. Formed in God's image by His hands, we live because of His very breath, the breath of God, the eternal life of the everlasting Lord of all. Notwithstanding the fall of Adam, God has purposed always to live in intimacy with man and He has poured out the treasure of heaven to assure it.

He made us His unique handiwork. He created us, not out of His need, but out of His great desire. We are made to worship, love and fellowship with Him in a very intimate way. I submit that there is no other act that brings more pleasure to God than when we crawl up in Abba's lap and sit in His embrace, yearning to hear His voice and proclaim back to Him, "Thanks, Daddy, for the way You love me and treat me in such a special way. I want to learn to love just like You love me. I want to be just like You when I grow up."

We can speak and sing with the tongues of angels, preach to thousands, run corporations and companies, influence millions for noble causes, but there is nothing we can do that pleases God like spending time with Him. Take some time today and every day to draw near and embrace Him. It feels good; it feels safe; it feels like Eden, it feels like home. And most of all, it makes God smile.

When is the last time you felt special? Did that feeling give you hope? How long will you wait to feel special again?

Scripture:

Genesis Chapter 1 and 2

Song to Consider: "In the Garden" - Charles A. Miles

Prayer: Abba, I come to embrace You with my thanks and my worship. There is none like You. No one can touch my heart like You do. No one can touch Your heart like me. Use this time to make me live, look, and love more like You. I rest in Your lap and declare this is my home, this is where I dwell. Being with You is what You made me for. I long to make You smile. For Jesus' sake, Amen.

Omega
(Conclusion)

Thanks for taking the time to read this book. Hopefully, you have heard my heart. My desire is that you realize, as I have, that the important things in life are wrapped in a relationship with this One, Jesus the Christ. He is the only way to know our Creator and the purposes for which He made us. In Him we live, and move, and have our significance. His calling is our highest purpose and the only purpose that will outlast our stay here.

I have encountered many along my path who find it hard to believe they are chosen. They find it hard to accept that forgiveness can cover their failures and wash away their guilt and shame; that it's never too late in life to choose a different path, a path that leads to joy and peace and everlasting love. These weren't people that did not believe in God. Indeed, many professed to believe in Jesus. Still, their lives were filled with remorse, apprehension and turmoil. I have, at times, been one of these folks.

God has offered abundant life through a relationship with Christ. We don't achieve this relationship by keeping rules, following creeds or hanging out with good people. We realize the abundant life God has promised by intentionally staying close to God and spending time with Him. It is a desire born in hearts that are grateful and motivated by love. It is power born in minds made alive and transformed by the Breath of Heaven. It is hope that rests in the child-like faith that Father loves us with the power of a divine affection; he loves not out of His need, but out of His immense desire to make us His own.

Once we come to the realization that we are chosen, forgiven and loved, we can be the instruments of God's love in the earth. Our hearts, no longer our own, are repurposed to display love, joy, peace, kindness and generosity that will change our world and the world of others around us. It is these gifts - not our rules - that bring a dramatic change in people's lives. These gifts are given to the down and out as well as the high and mighty. They work for princes and paupers alike. They wield great power in the hands of both children and the aged. Friends, there is no higher calling or nobler cause or greater joy known to man. There is no more powerful influence to change hearts, minds, families, churches, towns, and nations. Only those who are convinced the news is good can share the "Good News" with authenticity. The best advocates for change are the ones who themselves are changed. We are chosen, forgiven and loved. My prayer is that God, through Jesus, will seize you with the power of His divine affection so that you can experience the passion of His indescribable love today and have the confidence of being **Chosen, Forgiven and Loved.**

Sources Cited

Keller, Timothy. *The Freedom of Self-forgetfulness: The Path to True Christian Joy*. Chorley, England: 10Publishing, 2012. Print.

Manning, Brennan. *Ruthless Trust: The Ragamuffin's Path to God*. San Francisco: HarperSanFrancisco, 2000. Print.

Manning, Brennan. "Brennan Manning on God's Love." *Key Life*. Key Life Network, 14 Oct. 2011. Web. 3 June 2014.

Tozer, A. W., and Samuel Zwemer Marinus. *The Pursuit of God*. Harrisburg, PA: Christian Publications, 1948. Print.

Warren, Rick. "Love Is an Action." *Daily Hope*. Daily Hope Ministries, 21 May 2014. Web. 17 July 2014.